When Mimosas Bloom

For Mey — I've loved you since I landed in Perry! Thanks for honoring me with your presence!

Love, Lincoln

Susan B.

When Mimosas Bloom

Susan H. Lincoln

iUniverse, Inc.
New York Lincoln Shanghai

When Mimosas Bloom

iUniverse books may be ordered through booksellers or by contacting:

iUniverse
2021 Pine Lake Road, Suite 100
Lincoln, NE 68512
www.iuniverse.com
1-800-Authors (1-800-288-4677)

Because of the dynamic nature of the Internet, any Web addresses or links contained in this book may have changed since publication and may no longer be valid.

The views expressed in this work are solely those of the author and do not necessarily reflect the views of the publisher, and the publisher hereby disclaims any responsibility for them.

ISBN: 978-0-595-46763-1 (pbk)
ISBN: 978-0-595-91057-1 (ebk)

Printed in the United States of America

This book is dedicated to the region from which I come, and the people who have loved me throughout my growing up and my growing old(er). May the joys of "growing up Southern—surrounded by family and friends," be shared by the readers who find their way to these pages.

When I count my blessings, you're all there … every one of you.

Special blessings to the husband, the daughter and the son, as well as the mother who developed a fear of visiting us because of everything I had written about her. "Someone may recognize me," she always said, and my other family members share her pain.

When I scream, "Technical support!?!?," Mark Viola comes running … and I'm grateful. There were "readers" who checked for spelling and punctuation errors, so if you find any, please tell Angela, Frank, Beth or David. So many people were instrumental in bringing this book to reality. But my newspaper audiences deserve greater accolades for "bringing me up right," and correcting me when I was wrong. I'm fortunate to be an only child, and to have such a large family.

Contents

Little Phone on the Prairie

'Tis The Season To Be Jolly

Thou Shalt Not Whine

Boy, Oh Boy!

We Gather Together

Mothers Only Rest When They're Dead

*Growing
Up
Southern*

My Best Secret

It was during 11 a.m. worship on Father's Day, 2005, that I realized my father had been dead for 25 years.

I could believe 10 or 15, but 25? It hardly seems possible.

In the midst of the preacher's stories about his father and other fathers, I remembered some of my own, and it was fitting that my mind was wandering on this Sunday morning because it was meandering back to another sanctuary, on Ft. Dale Road in Greenville, Ala., where many memories of my father originate.

Actually, many of my own memories are entwined along the staircases of that church building which I knew like the back of my hand. It was a large building, and loomed even larger in the imagination of a child. The sanctuary would seat 500 though we rarely had more than half that many, except on Easter. The classrooms, which attached to the church always intrigued me, for they sat there perfectly furnished, waiting for someone to play the piano or to color on the stacks of paper. When the crowds left by 12:10 p.m. on Sundays, these rooms were strangely quiet and strangely inviting.

We were always there, you see. My father was church treasurer, which meant that as everyone rushed for the best tables in downtown restaurants or visited in the parking lot, we tramped down the stairs toward the office annex to lock up the money in the safe.

I am not using the term "we" loosely. As a child, I don't ever recall not being in my father's presence for this financial responsibility. From white patent shoes to black patent shoes, I was right beside him or right behind him.

Since my father waited for all the people to empty the sanctuary before collecting the offering plates beside the massive arrangement of gladioli (always gladioli), I had time to saunter through the whole building—noticing the crafts left on small tables, the wastebaskets filled with Dixie cups and empty jars which once held apple juice, as well as the uninteresting, green rooms occupied by adults with only a table surrounded by chairs. My dad checked every entrance to make sure the doors were locked, and there were at least 10. That's when I went around the building, noticing the organist's shoes, the sterling silver donated by a prominent family in the memorial room, the Southern Baptist Convention-generated prints of Jesus scattered throughout.

My great grandfather was in a framed picture of an earlier congregation, and I often stopped by the library to look at it. The library was usually hot; the kitchen was always cold. Life was very predictable when I was 8.

When we finally found our way through the maze of hallways and staircases to the church office, an inner office held the safe which looked like it might have seen Jesse James in an earlier day. It was a substantial piece of steel in army green, with sleek detailing around the four corners. When our job was done, we would jump in the blue Chevrolet (always a blue Chevrolet) and sit around our kitchen table eating a roast which had spent its morning in a pressure cooker while we were in church.

I never will forget the Sunday that my father was talking over me and the green beans, to my mother, about a church matter and how no one else had access to the safe.

"Eighty to the right, sixty to the left, forty to the right, 20 to the left, zero to the right, and click!" I said, as if I was doing a magic show.

Mother pretty much disregarded the show, but my father was captivated. He paused, mid-bite, and said nothing while staring in my direction.

Mother caught on pretty quickly and asked, "What are those numbers?"

"That's the combination to the church safe," said I, proud that I could count by 20s and remember the appropriate direction too.

I'm sure by Monday at 8 a.m., the wheels were in motion to change the combination to the church safe. And from that day forward, I had limited access to the inner sanctum which held the tithes and the offerings; I was allowed, instead, to sit in the secretary's swirling chair and long for the day when I had my own tape dispenser and stapler.

Shortly after that fateful Sunday, when I broke into song using the church combination as my musical score, my mother took me aside and tempted me with perfection.

"That needs to be your best secret," she said, winking. "Don't ever say it aloud."

So I never told anyone, until today. And now it unlocks nothing, but some steel-clad memories which are worth more to me, than anything that safe ever held.

A Waltz and a Candy Bar

In a mesmerizing way, I was back on the piano stool yesterday as the metronome in my head ticked away 30 years.

The nine-year-old daughter began piano lessons.

And I remembered mine.

This transition into the world of piano is a rite of passage for women in my family. It was assumed that you would take piano lessons and, thus, be obligated to play for the family at Christmas and reunions.

What a pressure cooker.

I recall that my mother and her two sisters took piano from a traveling music professor who came to rural towns during the summer months and taught the culturally deprived.

My mother still plays a ditty or two, and her sisters play a ditty or two, but the music professor never stayed long enough to produce an accomplished musician. That's why they signed up all the girl children in their respective families for weeks upon weeks of piano lessons, stretching into years upon years.

I was a five-year investment although my skills don't reflect the time involved.

I flinched when Sunday afternoon get-togethers of my childhood spawned a "Susan, play the piano for us." I was, after all, obliged to do so. My parents had paid for lessons.

My father would have busted a button with pride had I ever progressed to the front of the church to play the piano or organ, but God spared me that horror by surrounding me with highly talented peers who were motivated to assume those positions of leadership.

I will be forever grateful.

Still, my finest moments on the piano come when I finally empty the house of children and husband.

Then I pull out the stool, sweep the tail of my tuxedo jacket over the piano bench in Liberace fashion, and play to my heart's content. Time becomes irrelevant, as I remember the axiom, "Music washes the dust off of ordinary life."

That is why I've enrolled the daughter in lessons. A rite of passage, yes. A tradition, yes. Something she wants to do, yes. And an opportunity to wash the dust off of ordinary life.

In my piano lessons of yore, gold stars were affixed to music when you became especially proficient at "Jingle Bells" or "Swan Lake." Gold stars begat Pay Day candy bars. And if you earned a certain quantity of such stars and bars, you were presented with a plastic bust of Mozart or Beethoven or Bach.

My mother still has these great musicians in a closet with the Barbie dolls. Mozart and Ken in the closet. What a vision.

"Practice makes perfect," I told the daughter … and so the nine-year-old has begun her musical journey with a zeal for practice. When the husband arrived home for dinner, I announced glibly that we needed to build a music studio in the rear of the property…. "where she could concentrate."

"What?" he said, as "Bingo" was played over, and over, and over.

One day, when her children are absent from her home, she'll pull out the piano bench and entertain herself, playing confidently and courageously. Then she will thank me appropriately.

And, if she's like her mother and learns this important lesson at the beginning, she'll reward herself with a Pay Day candy bar.

I'll just bet Mozart did, too.

Imagine that

Waving an oddly bent coat hanger covered with foil, my friend Frances was a princess who ruled from the wrap-around porch of her family's home.

She wore a flowing housedress, a scarf tied around her head and flowers in her hair.

I played, reservedly, watching her cautiously.

My friend Laura tamed all the wild animals in our neighborhood, calling them from the highest limb in the closest tree. She saw lions and tigers and bears, oh my, while saving the rest of us from bodily harm.

"I saved your life," she would declare loudly from a poplar tree, but the only potential predator I ever saw was an occasional blue jay.

I just shook my head.

Then there was my friend Becky who said she had Jesus in her attic.

This one really bothered me.

I said, "If Jesus did come back, what makes you think he'd pick your attic?"

Oh ye of little faith.

My mother whispered softly to Frances' mother: "I'm afraid Susan doesn't have much imagination."

I was pretty sure that statement was a well-intended personality assessment, and not a criticism, but I never had the courage to question her about it. From that day on, however, I tried to have an imagination.

When everybody else laid on the grass and saw puppy dogs and dinosaurs in the cloud shapes above, I mostly just saw clouds. But I would suggest a shape or two, and those with imagination never saw what I saw.

I took great pride in that. It was about time for them to get a dose of their own medicine.

The most troubling times came when visiting readers showed up in my elementary classrooms and invariably suggested, "Now close your eyes, and imagine yourself ..."

When I closed my eyes, I saw mostly dark with some squiggly things which might indicate a vision problem. I could never see myself on a magic carpet, or on top of the Eiffel tower.

It just didn't make sense. I knew I was in Alabama and my parents couldn't possibly afford to travel to the Eiffel Tower.

A shortage of imagination still plagues me. The husband can visit the Civil War battlefields of Northern Virginia and re-live military maneuvers. I just like the quiet.

He sees the banks of the Aucilla River in Florida and finds the places Indians would have used as homesites, or envisions the wooly mammoths who roamed.

I just look around for snakes.

The fact is, I don't re-live history well. Shoot, I can hardly find the Big Dipper without help.

I have wondered if imagination, like the genetic tendency toward twins, skips a generation. One of my children had as many as six imaginary friends. I remember traveling with nine people in our vehicle, although I could only see three. One of them had a Muslim name which I still cannot explain.

I recall, too, the Sunday afternoon, when for the neighborhood girls, the son was a dog: a yapping, whimpering, on-four-legs dog. I smiled as I remembered Frances reigning with her coat hanger and Laura in her make-believe Africa.

I realized that my mother's careful prediction, "I'm afraid Susan doesn't have much imagination," was completely accurate. Still I prefer to believe that I have been endowed with the public trust: while everybody else around me is losing their wits, somebody needs to keep their head on straight.

Imagine that, if you can.

Little Store on the Prairie

If I was 35 years younger, it would be time to go to the little store.

Summer signaled the beginning of our frequent trips down the paved hill, through the shade of oak trees which canopied the street, around the corner, past those yapping dogs and then several blocks later, to the right where the little store stood.

It was white clapboard store with a tin sign which read, between the Coca-Cola symbols, Sikes Grocery.

We zoomed into the sidewalk entrance of that store on our Western Auto bikes which were always Christmas presents, and started digging in our pockets for the penny, the nickel or the dime we brought (depending on our mother's generosity or our own industriousness).

Walking into Sikes Grocery was like walking into the best of America. Mr. Sikes, a friendly fellow, greeted us heartily—clothed faithfully in denim overalls with a checkered shirt and a hat that advertised John Deere, Caterpillar or some other manufacturer. It was a small store, but I remember eyeing it from top to bottom: the ice chests on top with a grill or maybe two, and some camouflage hunting wares; the next level displaying toilet tissue, a dusty jar of mayonnaise, a few boxes of cereal, some detergent and cans of soup; dog food in bags on the floor level, with charcoal and a couple of barrels to sit upon. In the corner were hampers of fresh vegetables and stalks of sugar cane, when in season.

The greatest treasures, however, were before us. Mr. Sikes' corner in the store was surrounded by a U-shaped layout of glass-topped freezers which held ice cream delights, my favorite being an orange sherbet push-up. Seven cents.

On top of the counter were, of course, bandanas in red and blue, lighters and refills, pocket knives and sunglasses, but we focused on those large, clear glass jars which held mountains of candy, for a penny and up. Your life became a happy event with one-cent bubblegum, one-cent peppermint, one-cent pixie sticks filled with colored sugar. With a nickel, you felt privileged. A dime, and you were royalty.

There were pickles, of course, and pickled eggs or pigs' feet, but we merely viewed those as if we were in a museum, not as serious consumers. If we were going to eat a pig's feet, it would be at our mothers' mandate, not of our own free will.

So we looked instead toward the gingerbread cookies iced in pink, and sold in a wax paper packages; candy bars in all-American wrappers, best enjoyed with those 6 oz. bottled drinks which came out of the freezers that encircled Mr. Sikes.

I didn't think life got much better than this.

And I might have been right.

The decision-making process was a tedious one, with much agony and emotional wrestling. Mr. Sikes viewed it amicably, not rushing, not pushing. He was a parent, but he didn't act like one; he was a grandparent, and he acted more like that. He looked at us from underneath his drug store glasses and watched as we analyzed life-changing decisions, like the pixie stick over the bubblegum. Then he paused patiently as we counted pennies.

"Thank you very much, little lady," he would say, and each individual's purchase was carefully placed in a small brown bag.

We left the store and I'll never forget the snap of that screened door. Wooden doors had a more final slam than today's aluminum doors. Wooden doors let you know that someone had come, and someone had gone. We had gone, and left behind that door with its tin Colonial bread sign across the middle that bid us welcome during summer's long days.

Without saying a word, we knew the routine. We bicycled to the end of that street, turned left and headed straight to the biggest oak tree around. There, we tilted our bikes against the curb and sat in the shade to enjoy our purchase. It was the forerunner to lunch-with-the-girls or bridge club. "What are we going to do today?" would always come up and the answers began emerging: dolls or house, fort or war, build a club house, paint a birdhouse, climb trees, play beauty parlor or school, conduct church or funeral services. The groans and cheers that each suggestion garnered led to the final decision. You could protest, but it was best to realize that you lived in America where the majority rules.

Great lessons were learned in the summertime amid sprinklers and lemonade, fireworks and June bugs, tree houses and watermelon in the backyard.

Many of them came from our trips to the little store where the Coca-Cola thermometer registered 90-something degrees, and men lingered on wooden barrels for refreshing drinks and talk, as children visited once or twice a day with pennies in their pockets and plans in their heads.

Today, everybody wants a super store.

I want a little one.

Stained Glass Reflections

Sunday when I sat in the church pew, my feet touched the floor.

It wasn't always so.

For I was in my home church of Greenville, Ala., to celebrate its 140th anniversary.

And for many years in my home church, my feet didn't touch the ground.

Literally and figuratively.

For individuals who don't have stained glass windows in their hearts and memories, this 140 years won't mean much.

But to me, as the organ resounded, I remembered walking that very long aisle. This church is the only thing in my memory which has grown larger with time.

My grandmother's house doesn't seem nearly as grand as it did in my childhood, and the hall to my first grade class is barely a stroll although it looked like a 10-mile path through the desert at six years old. Given those skewed recollections, I had decided that adult perceptions shrink all landmarks of our past. But it isn't so.

This church has grown.

"How in the world did I make it all the way down that aisle?" I wondered as the organist played background music for my thoughts. There have been some profound walks: the day I professed my faith before a fatherly old preacher, the day I prepared to bury my own father, and the day I said "I do."

Wonder how many people have walked that aisle in 140 years? How many were married, buried, welcomed to the "family of faith"?

Before I got too deep in thought, the organist and pianist began playing together "Victory in Jesus." We all stood and we sang all three verses, and

I did note that they had picked up the time considerably in the last 40 of those 140 years.

"Amazing Grace," of course, had to be next because you simply don't gather Baptists to talk about heritage without finding your way to "Amazing Grace."

Generations of young people gathered with parents and grandparents, to offer church memories, prayers, praise.

A soloist recalled through music the large impact that small tasks can have: "you taught me in Sunday School when I was 8 ... you showed me how to find Psalm 23 ... you led me to understand first the words, and then the meaning of 'Jesus Loves Me'."

The ending to this celebration, and the focus on the next 140 years, was brought by an aged, rambling preacher from Tennessee—the son of a Mississippi cotton farmer. He has among his parishioners now "tenant farmers, country music singers, well-known American political and literary figures, as well as average citizens and academic theologians."

He talked about Waylon, Willie and the boys. It was pleasurable preaching.

And yet he made me realize that stained glass windows can be found in the oddest places.

Which brought me right back to a quote which follows me around most of my days: "Without faith, we are all stained glass windows in the dark."

And without churches, it's just darker out there.

A Mimosa Tree:
a wonderful thing to own

The mimosa trees are blooming, and I am presumptuous enough to believe that they are blooming for me. That is because mimosa trees provided the setting for many of my childhood memories. And just as my mother predicted the advent of a new school year by the spider lilies which children once brought to her teacher's desk, I predicted the coming of cake and ice cream, and another birthday, because the mimosa trees were blooming.

As a child, I decorated mud pies with the bean pods and pink powder-puff blossoms that mimosa trees produce. My culinary expertise goes way back.

I also observed my cat's relationship with the mimosas, as she climbed the sprawling limbs of the three trees my father had planted in a triangular pattern, in the center of our backyard.

One day, I followed that cat up the tree.

Then every day, I followed that cat up the tree.

And soon, I spent more time in those trees than the cat. My parents were surely wondering why in the world a girl-child such as I would be so intrigued with a tree. But the reasons were many.

In the juncture formed by the branching trunks, I could read a book in comfort, if I carried along my Girl Scout sit-upon for cushioning. And I did.

I could make circular leis of flowers for my friends with the blooms. And I did. I could throw things at the boys below. And I did.

As a child, a mimosa was a wonderful thing to own.

Until I fell out of the top of one.

That's bad enough.

What I did after the fall is worse.

I had recently viewed an episode of "Mannix." You're probably too young to remember this flashy, dark-headed detective who always got his man. In one particular episode, a character fell from a tall building and suffered from amnesia.

As I lay on the ground with the world spinning around, I decided to suffer from amnesia, too. It was summertime; the living was easy. I needed excitement.

I remember wailing at the bottom of the mimosa trees, calling for Mama. (In my day, you called for Mama, not 911.)

She came racing out of the kitchen with her apron and her dishtowel, fearing the worst.

"You probably just got the breath knocked out of you," she said, hopefully.

But I was holding my arm close, which was a true injury, and whimpering a bit.

Then I vividly, and with deep regret, remember gazing blankly into the blue Alabama sky and muttering in a faraway voice, "Where am I?" and "What happened?".... just as they had done on "Mannix."

This is probably the most shameful thing I ever did. I must have been really good at it, too, because the next thing I knew, I was in the back seat of her maroon Rambler heading toward the doctor's office, at speeds exceeding the legal limit.

Of course, by that time, I was confessing mightily that I knew where I was, and where we were going, and it really wasn't necessary because I was fine and there was no reason to worry.

Clearly, this was no time to bring up "Mannix."

I tried again, quietly and calmly, "Hey, Mama, I'm really fine now. I did get the breath knocked out of me, and things were going 'round and 'round, but I know where I am now, and I'm just fine."

"We'll let Dr. Dunklin determine that," she said.

My father met us there, and I was wishing in a big way to be struck by genuine amnesia.

Dr. Dunklin must have seen that same episode of "Mannix," for he quickly disregarded any amnesia, and looked at the arm which was bruised, maybe sprained, but was going to be fine. Probably $35, thank you very much.

I don't remember my mother being very jovial on the way home. I do remember being restricted from those mimosa trees while my arm healed. Soon thereafter, as I outgrew mimosas, natural predators invaded their bark and my father handled that situation and my mother by having the mimosas chain-sawed out of our lives.

I feel partly responsible.

I recall, again with regret, waiting for several months before confessing all the details of the sordid event. Fortunately, the God of forgiveness smiled upon me and gave my parents more mercy than I should have experienced. I promised never, ever for the rest of my life to feign illness, and I have kept that promise with the memorable whir of a chainsaw in the distance.

My parents' extravagant mercy should, of course, make me more merciful.

But I declare, if my children ever fabricate such an illness, their only hope of redemption is for me to, indeed, be struck with amnesia leaving me no recollection of their folly.

When you see a mimosa tree, you probably don't give it a second thought.

When mimosas bloom.... I don't say, "Where am I?" or "What happened?" For I remember all the times well, and most of them, fondly.

*The
Serpent
in the
Garden*

Boiled Okra

It was a night when I deserved an hour of solitude, an escape from the remainder of the house and its occupants, a little peace and quiet, and lavender.

So after starting the washing machine, the clothes dryer and the dishwasher, I escaped up 13 stairs to the bathroom that might irreverently be referred to as my inner sanctuary. I'm an only child and I don't share well. But my bathroom: I don't share at all.

Lavender bath bubbles had been among the gifts of Christmas, and I was about to enjoy the bounty.

I've always enjoyed a hot bath—so hot that your skin turns red and you feel sick when you get out. That's a good bath.

On that night, while steam rose from the bubbles, I sunk down into the water that I was sure had curative powers. Minutes later, I wanted more hot water. As I moved to turn the faucet, a small green lizard crawled off a bath sponge of the same color.

I didn't jump or scream. I chose to be calm. I like the green lizards—not in my bath, mind you—but as a general rule, I co-exist with them better than those skinks-from-hell which look like snakes.

"How did you get in here?" I asked the lizard and he didn't reply. I looked up and around, for any crevice which might have allowed him entry. I had brought no plants in this second-story bathroom, and I was clueless about his point of entry.

"I'll get the boys to get him out when I'm through," I decided, going for one more curative dip while keeping an eye upon the uninvited guest.

"I usually bathe alone," I told the lizard, and he looked at me so curiously. It must be nice to be cute and well-dressed 24 hours a day. When he cocked his head, he looked like the Geico gecko which has become a favor-

21

ite creature we all admire. I'm not sure I would have been surprised if this lizard had addressed me with a British accent.

Instead, he lost his footing and fell in the tub with me.

I was no longer calm, because he was swimming around like a mad lizard, trying to find his way out of this watery mire.

"Aiiiihhhhh," I screamed mightily, standing up with bubbles all over me.

"Get out," I screamed again.

"Help me," I screamed a third time.

Down below, the 24-hour news channel, coupled with three running appliances and a Play Station 2, obscured any idea of mutiny from this deep tub.

Moments later, the lizard's furious breast stroke became a motionless float.

"Oh my God," I said to only God, I suppose. "He's dead in my bath water."

Then I realized he was probably boiling, so I grabbed my tube of bath gel and used it as a little life preserver. As soon as I got it within reach of the little green fellow, he climbed aboard and I placed him on the side of the tub.

I was breathing furiously, but he was breathing more furiously. As I sat back and wondered what he had done in my water, I saw his chest heaving back and forth, while simultaneously, his eyes were shifting left and right, and his spiffy, chartreuse green had boiled into a cooked-okra look. In fact, he did look like a skinny, cooked okra, with eyes and a heartbeat.

I studied him carefully, wondering if he would die right there before me. I observed that his tail was twice as long as his short body. He sat there stunned, as did I, afraid to move. We were in a motionless stand-off for minutes. Finally, he got his breath and scurried up the side of a picture frame—I think he had that sick feeling you get when you take a bath that's too hot.

"It's not good for you," I said to him, having had the same words said to me before.

Trying not to alert the lizard, I began draining the water and inching toward a towel before he saw the towel and liked it a lot since it was deep forest green. I wondered if my bathroom reminded him of a tropical rainforest he had heard about, or if it just reminded him of hell.

After fully clothing, and watching him carefully move from picture frame, to bath products, to a green candle he could love, I went to the loft and announced to the husband: "I nearly died in that tub and no one came to check on me."

"It's not good to take a bath that hot," he said.

I just shook my head and remembered why I needed that bath so badly.

"A lizard fell in the tub with me," I said as a spicy retort, and he looked up but didn't move.

"I need you to come get him," I pleaded.

"Is he clean?" the husband asked, laughing at his cleverness.

If that lizard had had a British accent, I might have kept him ... as my second husband.

Be Careful When You Say It:
I need a bug light

After weeks of living at the mercy of mosquitoes brought about by high water, I think the God of the North Wind accomplished what we feeble and frail humans in Florida were unable to do.

He annihilated them.

Or swatted them toward a warmer climate.

Or gave them hiding places until the sun could shine.

Who knows?

But in the midst of this temporary and slight cold blast, we give thanks for the thousands upon thousands of mosquitoes—the state bird, you know—who packed their bikinis and headed to the tropics, taking their friends and family members with them.

I had tried a number of frontal assaults upon the insects which had come to call my home their own. "Everybody has to do their part," I told my family members. "So swat every one you see, remembering that those left standing will be the ones which bite you in the dark of the night."

We left lights on for the mosquitoes, in Tom Bodett fashion, trying to lure them to the opposite side of the house from where we were huddled against their attacks.

But they were too smart for that.

They could hear the door slam and the television play. They wanted to be a part of the family—blood relations, if you will. And in vampire fashion, they did try to hum their way into our hearts but it's hard to love someone who brings you nothing but pain and aggravation.

When I said that, the husband looked suspiciously at me as if I was disparaging him in front of the children. "Not you," I said. "I was speaking of the mosquitoes."

I noticed while ridding the porches of pollen and straw, that the electric leaf blower did a pretty fair job of disorienting the insects, and I left it out in the garage in case the children wanted to inflict pain and hardship upon these mosquitoes.

"Well, we can't exactly walk around with leaf blowers," said the daughter, always concerned with How Things Look.

"Your choice," I said, as I knocked a mosquito off her head and she slapped at one on her leg.

I also decided that it was time to buy a new bug light since the existing one was losing its zzzzzzt power, and these New Generation mosquitoes were more than it could handle. They have done aerobics and now know karate.

"We must do our part," I reiterated to the family, because neighbors to our left and right were electrocuting mosquitoes by the thousands and the few stragglers who survived were limping into our yards, with their needle-like stingers poised for revenge. The aging bug light couldn't keep up with the refugee flow.

So I jumped in the car, killed the mosquitoes who followed me into its interior (they are everywhere) and headed toward town. The grill on my vehicle was layered with dead mosquito bodies, which will only be removed in time for the onslaught of love bugs.

I noticed standing water on the left side of the road and the right. "Is the water going down any?" I asked myself and I couldn't come up with a sure answer.

Not knowing where the bug lights stayed, I entered the local hardware store, found someone in a red vest and announced, "I need a bug light."

There was silence among the nuts and bolts.

The men shifted their eyes left and right, trying not to look at each other.

What? I wondered. I checked my zipper; it was in the correct position. Did I forget to dress? What was it?

Finally, a friend from long ago broke the ice and cleared the air for the working men who didn't know what to do with me. "If you want a Bud Light, you're in the wrong place," he said.

"Not a Bud Light," I said vehemently.

"A bug light."

"Ohhhhh, ohhhhh, ohhhhh," they said in unison with red vests snickering, red vests smiling and red vests pointing toward the proper aisle. Finally, a female of the species delivered me from the banter among the red vests and showed me the bug lights.

Since then, I've been working on my articulation.

And my annihilation

And my appreciation.

Circulation Problems

In the newspaper parking lot each day, I take roll: who's here, who's not.

When the husband was out of town to return the eldest child to college, I parked and locked my car while counting the others beside it. We were down three and a half employees. In a newspaper as small as ours, that's huge.

Yet I understood my role as team captain, and was confident that we could prevail. After all, we had a paper to get out. It didn't matter how long it took, we had to do it.

So I braced myself, clutched the back door knob and walked into the storage room where the lighting is dim. Just as I grabbed the second doorknob to enter the brightness and hum of newspaper work, I heard a shrill scream.

"Oh God," I said aloud.

It occurred to me at that moment, to turn around and drive—anywhere—just drive. But I like these people and I couldn't just desert them. Or could I?

I opened the door to see customers in the front office, and one particularly loquacious one. Perhaps they were just laughing, I told myself, and about that time, a blonde employee rushed toward me, whispering loudly, "It's a rat."

I knew she wasn't slandering someone's character; it had to be a four-legged creature.

"Oh joy," I said, smiling. With that same pageant smile plastered on my face, I asked, "Do the customers know?"

"No," she said holding on to my shoulders to keep herself from going over the edge. It seems our circulation manager was beating the circulation out of the rodent in the publisher's front office.

"With the door closed," she said.

"Well, why is the particularly loquacious customer laughing so loudly in the front office?" I then asked.

"Because another customer just blessed us out and he witnessed the whole thing," she said.

It was just another day in the salt mines.

I spoke to everyone in a guarded fashion as I approached my office and heard the circulation manager at work next door. He then departed with the lifeless rodent in a garbage bag, and trying to be discreet, did not announce his departure. So when he ran into the blonde, while holding the garbage bag, she screamed bloody murder and ran in the opposite direction.

I calmly spoke to the customers in the front office and explained, "She's a little high strung."

That's when the second rodent scampered by, unbeknownst to those who were gathered. Everyone raised eyebrows and exchanged looks. I tried to get the front office population out on the streets again and did very well except for a kind and friendly woman who asked, "What are you feeding that thing? He sure looks healthy."

Most of the staff screamed and ran in the opposite direction; I retreated to my office like a fearless leader and offered a safe haven to two others. After all, this was clearly a matter for the circulation manager.

The friendly female customer said, "I was raised on a farm and can kill it for you."

"Oh no," I said. "Please let me help you finish your business here."

"Honey, it's okay," she said.

The mouse (or rat, given your perspective) rushed through the office, under the graphic artist's chair with his hair blowing in the breeze, she reports.

Right behind him were three strong men with brooms and other weapons. He lived only briefly; they still survive.

"It happens," said the husband by phone, rather matter-of-factly. "It's an early 1900s building that doesn't seal up well, and on top of that, we buy newsprint by the ton and then stack newspapers in every corner. It happens—it just hasn't happened in a long time."

"Why doesn't it happen when you're here?" I asked, still wasting time on the big questions of life.

It had been like a House of Horrors: a scream here, a scream there. Deafening quiet and then a scream again.

Then a wonderful thing happened: the customer with no fear of rodents returned with a gift bag of assorted chocolates. "It's a good day for chocolate," she said, and no one argued.

Suddenly, the office was back to normal, or perhaps I should say it was business as usual. People came and went, and we haven't seen a four-legged creature since. Of course, that might be because the circulation manager attempted to dry up the rodents' circulation with poison placed at vantage points throughout the building.

In college, they teach you that circulation has to do with the distribution of newspapers throughout a community, but as it turns out, the man with that title at our office holds a broom … and our admiration.

Worm Guts for Mother's Day

"Are those worm guts on your hands?" I asked the son as I was about to pass him a sandwich.

"I'm pretty sure I washed 'em," he said.

"I think you'd better try again," I suggested.

"Those worm guts are hard to get off your hands," added the husband, shaking his head.

I just grimaced at the whole room. This is not the way it was supposed to be. I grew up watching sitcoms of normal families like the Cleavers and the Ricardos. The mother was always crisply dressed, had a tablecloth on the table, and was serving a nutritionally sound meal.

What a disappointment am I.

"Did you wear insect repellent?" I asked and the son answered in the affirmative.

"Do you have any homework?" I then inquired, as I whisked through the room, picking up stacks of mail and homeless socks.

Our conversations aren't even normal. I can hear June Cleaver asking now in a lilting voice, "So what did you do at school today, Beaver?"

Beaver, though freckled-faced and 100 percent boy, would report on someone's behavior and end his report with a polite "yes ma'am," all the while keeping his hands in his lap upon his linen napkin.

If I ask the question, I get a "Nothing" as the answer, unless there was a fight at school that day; the boy can always remember the fights.

So my life is reduced to Plenty Questions:

Do you have money in your lunchroom account?

Do you have baseball practice after school?

Did you do your homework?

Brush your teeth?

Comb your hair?

Wash your face?

Remember your binder?

Find your shoes?

Feed your dog?

Turn in your field trip money?

In my defense as we complete another celebration of Mother's Day, let me say that these questions are just another way of saying, "I love you."

I can hear the son challenge me now with a terse, "What?"

The point is, we aren't the Cleavers; we can't even be their bad neighbors. We are a flawed family of four, trying to stress education, health, cleanliness and godliness.

However feebly.

Motherhood, in reality, is much different from Fantasy Motherhood. I, too, grew up with a baby doll. I believed I would be adored by husband and children alike—revered as the hub of their wheel and the center of their universe.

I watched Kodak's "portrait of your lives" and saw those mothers in gauzy white gowns with clean, smiling babies. Those pictures haunted me during six weeks of colic, some 20 years ago.

In Fantasy Motherhood, there are no shouting matches, there are no broken bones, there are no generation gaps. There is love and communication.

In Reality Motherhood, there are jock straps and worm guts.

I miss Fantasy Motherhood and that clean baby doll, but my life has been enriched by…. worm guts.

Our mornings are rather quiet during the school term, as the son stumbles through breakfast and school preparations, and bids me a subdued farewell on his way to, well "prison," he would say: six hours in the same building, surrounded by books. He looks like a condemned young man.

Last week, as he left for higher education, I noticed one shoe untied, and he was loaded down with books and a baseball bag, so I simply motioned for him to stop as I bent down to remedy the untied shoe.

That's when the dog, in her effort to enrich my life too, put a dead squirrel right under my nose as I crouched down on my all fours. I lost my balance, but she held on tightly to the squirrel, dangling it above my flat-on-the-back body.

It was the happiest morning of the boy's school year. He and the husband laughed all the way to town.

I, the mother, made that happen and all it took was a dead squirrel.

Take that, June Cleaver.

Open Season on Frogs

A remarkable new pastime has leapt into my life, announcing its presence with a wide-mouthed ribbit.

It is open season on frogs in our neighborhood; enter at your own risk, because if you're green and jump around a lot, you could be next.

I know, deep in my heart, that frogs are plentiful and will reproduce. I know frog legs have been offered at restaurants as delicacies.

But it's a whole different pond when you talk about eating frogs who have been your neighbors. I have always preferred to purchase meat on Styrofoam, covered with plastic wrap, and emblazoned with the government's stamp of FDA approval, even if it means nothing.

I have, however, learned to eat the fish of the sea, the birds of the air, and the deer of the woods, for I am now surrounded by men who enjoy the hunt.

Once, at a restaurant with linen cloths, I ate frog legs and found them quite palatable. "But I'm not cooking them," I said to the husband and the son.

"I'll cook'em," said the husband who makes a grander mess than I.

"Wouldn't your friend like them for supper?" I asked the son.

Just then, the telephone rang. It was the friend's mother. "I don't want those frog legs; don't send them back here."

"We can't just waste them," said the son and I was glad to see some glimmer of responsibility for we've always said, you catch and release, or you catch and you eat. You don't just kill for the fun of it.

I could now prepare to choke on those words.

The friend's father had cleaned the frogs—about 20 of them—to a fare-thee-well, and I had prepared a lovely salad which would suffice as my meal if I chose to leap over the entree that evening.

In two local cookbooks, we looked for frog leg recipes and found none. I finally pulled out the heavy artillery of cookbooks, The Joy of Cooking. "If it's not in here, it's not meant to be cooked," I said to the husband, hoping beyond hope that no recipes existed.

But they were there—several of them, for fried frog legs and braised frog legs. There was even an introductory paragraph about frog legs—how they tasted—and that they might jump when you cooked them.

"That's it," I said. "I can't do this."

The plan (and there's always a plan), was for the husband to leave the baseball park, where we currently spend all waking hours, to rush home to fry those legs. He's a leg man, you know.

The plan (and there's always a plan), changed, as plans are apt to do. He was needed over the grill at the ballpark and the son was intent on the frog legs—had invited a neighborhood contingent over—so I marched myself home and pretended I was the bravest woman on earth. I often do this.

As I washed them for a second time and dried them carefully, I noted how much they looked like frog legs. "Just yesterday," I told myself, "they were hopping around from lily pad to lily pad …"

The batter was specific and required three bowls, so you dipped from egg wash, to bread crumbs, to parmesan cheese. And then the legs had to dry on my counter for 25-45 minutes so that the batter would be a "bound batter" for cooking.

It looked like a slaughterhouse with frog parts all over the counters. I was afraid the preacher might visit.

That salad was beginning to look better and better.

I heated the oil and awaited the red light to assure me of its adequacy for the task. At that moment—as an act of God, I'm sure—the headlights of the truck appeared and two men entered my house, craving legs. The husband dropped the frog parts in the oil and got to watch them jump, while I busied myself with other less important tasks.

"Let's eat," was voiced. We passed the cheese grits and the French bread, and then everybody took a pair of legs. I waited while the husband and the son risked their lives. I knew the husband would fake ecstasy to influence me, but the son isn't that savvy. "Wow," the boy said, "that's good."

I tried my set, and then another, and then the third, and decided that frog legs can be very good, indeed, even when they emerge from neighborhood ponds.

The phone rang. It was the daughter in college who doesn't care for fish, and doesn't particularly like venison or dove, and really just wants mainstream food which is purchased from a licensed restaurateur. (It must be genetic.)

"We're having frog legs," I said, waiting for her reaction.

"Arggh," she said. "I am sooo glad I'm not there."

"They're really are good," I said in defense. "But I, too, was skeptical."

"I'm going to the Japanese steak house tonight," she said.

"On a Monday night?" I asked. "Do you have the money for that?"

"They take the Tiger Card," she said, which means I have the money for that.

"Well, why don't you just eat peanut butter and jelly?" I asked. "It is a Monday night."

"I haven't been to the Japanese steak house in a long time," she said.

"I've only been once in my life," I countered.

"You should go more," she said. "It's great."

I hung up the phone and returned to my plate, which was piled with frog leg bones, and realized that as long as frogs are available, we'd better eat them.

So Marie Antoinette, and all her subjects, can eat cake.

Matters
of Life
and
Death

Give Me Your Chocolate,
and Nobody Will Get Hurt

"Life is like a box of chocolates."

On a park bench waiting for a bus, Forrest Gump made that statement famous and has left me to ponder it every Feb. 14 since.

His park bench wisdom probably explains my particular fondness for a Whitman's Sampler, which dutifully illustrates its contents. Every box of chocolates should be so kind.

If you want a nut nougat, you turn left. If you want a pecan cluster, look for the round one next to the venerable center spot, always held by the Whitman's Messenger. He brings pure, unadulterated chocolate, best enjoyed at room temperature.

I wish I craved apples, like Eve.

I wish I longed for yogurt or shredded wheat.

But it is chocolate that I crave, because it has been off-limits most of my life.

As a child, your mother typically explains that you shouldn't eat too much chocolate: it's too close to dinner, and all that sugar isn't good for you.

As a teenager, you're told to steer clear of chocolate for the all-important complexion issues which are terrorized by candy bars.

Then about the time you get that fixed, everything you eat begins to find its way to your hips, and you're told—once again—that chocolate is off limits or you'll pay mightily.

I want to know: when can you eat chocolate without anybody caring?

I don't know when, but I do know where: in the laundry room.

In my earlier, rebellious days, when I didn't want to share chocolate with the children (because it was too close to their dinnertime), and I didn't want the husband to see me eat it (because he doesn't long for chocolate and therefore can belittle my character weakness), I kept a stash in the laundry room. It was my pay, so to speak.

For every load I washed, I rewarded myself with a tiny piece of chocolate. After all, I had earned it, and nobody—but me—was going to find my chocolate next to the fabric softener. I didn't mind eating it in the presence of the washer and dryer; they never asked me to share.

Some say the months of the year were arranged with respect to the sun and the planets, but I believe it is chocolate which makes 365 days march by. Christmas brings chocolate fudge; Valentine's Day brings beautifully arranged collections of chocolate confections; the Easter Bunny brings chocolate with ears and eyes; I often receive chocolate for my birthday in June; and then I find myself in a dry spell, without chocolate.

Which reminds me of the shirt I first saw at a candy factory in Savannah, Ga. It was chocolate brown, of course, and it showed a desperate housewife declaring, "Give me your chocolate, and nobody will get hurt."

In a line-up, I'd say with certainty: it could be me.

Ellie Mae Goes to St. George Island

Come and listen to my story 'bout a man named Jed; a poor mountaineer, barely kept his family fed. Then one day, he was shooting at a coon, and up through the ground came a bubbling crude. Oil, that is. Black gold. Texas tea.

What happens next, in black-and-white, is the Clampetts moving lock, stock and barrel to Beverly Hills with granny's rocking chair strapped to the back of the pick-up.

My very own Ellie Mae will surely never forgive me for this, but we pulled a Clampett-style weekend at the beach.

And made our mark among the affluent.

Given the hurdles we jumped, most normal families would have decided against the weekend excursion. But when I think "beach," very little gets in my way. We've taken children who were sick. We've taken me sick. In a very real sense, the beach cures whatever is ailing me. I must go.

So when the reservationist told me, some five weeks ago, that the only thing available on St. George Island was a one-bedroom unit, I said "Okay."

The husband said, "What? The four of us in a one-bedroom? I'd just as soon stay home."

"It'll be fine," I assured him. "There's a pull-out sofa."

Until the day of departure, that husband-of-mine called daily hoping for a cancellation somewhere, anywhere.

There was no cancellation. There was a one-bedroom unit with our name on it, and we might as well be happy.

So we collectively decided to be happy.

41

That's when the water pump blew out on the Jeep. Hours before we were to leave, all the "doctors" in town doomed the Jeep to stay at home.

"We can't go?" the children whined.

"We'll take the truck," I said, confidently.

"All four of us in that little truck, and then in a one-bedroom?" the husband asked, and I think he might have cried. Ellie Mae was rolling her eyes.

But I vacuumed the floor mats, cleaned out two months' worth of wrappers and meeting minutes, and tried to keep a positive attitude.

"It's clean," I pronounced, and that's when the next black cloud moved over our heads.

Literally, a black cloud, and we had no cover for the back of the truck.

"We'd better go buy some garbage bags," the husband said, and I knew just what he meant.

The daughter did not. "Garbage bags?" she questioned. Then it hit her. "Oh no," she said.

Yes, we wrapped every suitcase in a big, black garbage bag, piled on the fishing rods, the inner tubes, the ice chest, the tackle boxes and away we bounced down the highway.

"We look like we're going to the dump," Ellie Mae said in deep anxiety, and I couldn't disagree.

Two short hours later, when the backseat boy and girl were complaining about cramped quarters and difficulty breathing, we pulled into the parking lot of our one-bedroom and took most of our garbage bag luggage upstairs (quickly before anyone noticed).

"We'll just leave the rest," said the husband. "Nobody would think we have anything worth stealing," and he was right. Parked next to a black Lexus with a moon roof, we looked like the cleaning crew and there's some security in that.

So we ate, drank and were merry, in our small truck, with our one bedroom, and one humiliated child. And just as I suspected, the weekend cured everything.

Even the water pump.

Hanging on a Chandelier

When your aunt, with the chandelier in her bathroom, dies ... all of life is diminished.

Aunt Lucy was a favorite—for me and for many of my cousins.

She never married and never got stodgy.

Instead, she wore what looked like an entire jewelry store's inventory, and shoes that matched any outfit.

She was 85 when she died.

A graduate of Auburn University in Auburn, Ala., she was recently honored by that college when it celebrated its centennial for the admission of women. One hundred women of note were honored during this 100th anniversary.

Aunt Lucy became synonymous with all-things-Auburn for our family, and many were poised to attend the always-open party at her house when football action kicked off.

But instead, family members found themselves at the funeral home.

When I got the news by telephone, I immediately flashed back to the chandelier in her bathroom. It wasn't a ballroom chandelier, but to someone six years old, it was impressive. We certainly didn't have chandeliers in our bathrooms at home, I keenly observed.

On the two-hour drive from her home to ours, I remember announcing, "One day, I'm gonna have a chandelier in my bathroom."

I know now it will have to be a bathroom the husband doesn't frequent, for he would never understand.

My observations continued as the will was read. She wasn't a wealthy woman, but she was a generous one: trinkets are being distributed to all family members, then to everyone 16 and over in the United States. There will be some left over.

Recently, when I reflected upon Aunt Lucy's influence, I realized I had previously written about her role in our family and its annual reunion: "While Aunt Mattie Faye is calling everybody by name, Aunt Lucyle is paying the children quarters to fan the older family members because it is a broiling 101 degrees in the shade.

"She's also financially supporting the family portrait which is taken of the 75 or so family members who gather each year. She's the family benefactor of sorts, always sending gifts, always sending love, always telling you how cute you are. Half the troubled kids in New York would be teaching Sunday School if they'd had an Aunt Lucy to tell them how cute they were."

There was a profound sadness at the time of her death.

Then, within the next week, the cover on my bathroom light fixture fell off.

I think it was a sign.

I need a chandelier in my bathroom. Some purple shoes. A bracelet or twelve.

They certainly can't replace Aunt Lucy, but they can remind me of her. Fondly.

Even an Orange Boiled Egg Tastes White

Every year, about this time, I have an uncontrollable urge to boil eggs.

It happens when azaleas and dogwoods bloom, girls wear frilly dresses and bonnets, and boys do whatever boys do for the other 11 months of the year, minus a shirt.

I knew the urge was coming last week when I observed the lunch of a neighbor's gardener. He had a large, cold drink; a larger, plastic cup of ice; and two boiled eggs, to accompany his sandwich and fruit.

I almost asked him for one of those eggs.

For eggs, in my Mother's book, were a staple. She survived the Depression and grew up eating eggs for breakfast every morning, before they learned the word cho-les-ter-ol. Recently, a doctor told her she needs to quit eating those eggs because she ate enough to last her a lifetime … before she was 30.

But when she's feeling really gamey and no one's looking, she boils one. If it's Saturday night and she has nowhere to go, she may fry one. Who will know?

Boiled eggs were once staples in my lunchbox, either before lock-top bags were invented or before my mother agreed to invest in them (and rinse them out). Instead, she'd wrap that boiled egg in wax paper, and put a rubber band around it to keep the wrap secure. After I threw my lunch box around in the car, in the hallway, and in my locker, the egg looked like it needed a plastic surgeon.

But with a little salt and pepper, it was Easter all over again.

Since boiled eggs rarely appear on our landscape, my children probably won't need to worry about cholesterol. But if nutritionists discover that cereal is detrimental to your health, we're all in trouble.

Even though they aren't a favorite, we started the ritual boiling of eggs this year, our personal way of ushering in spring: twelve for Tuesday, all pink and blue, and orange, and marbleized purple. "This is fun," said the littlest one. "Can I have one with my lunch?"

"Why sure," I said, "But I'm not sure you really like boiled eggs. You didn't care for them the last time I fixed one for you."

"But it was white," he said.

"Well, the orange one is going to taste the same," I assured him.

"No, the other one was white," he maintained.

"But when we take the shell off this one, it will be white too," I explained.

"It'll be fine," he said, patting me on the hand.

I peeled the shell and handed the smooth and slippery egg to him. "I'm really glad you like boiled eggs," I said as he took his first bite.

His first bite returned.

"It tastes like the white one," he said with such disappointment.

I retrieved the remains and looked fondly upon the three-quarters of a boiled egg which was left.

"It's been a long time since I had a boiled egg," I told myself, so I sat down and partook. Then I looked longingly at the other 12 sitting so pretty in Easter grass.

I think I could have eaten half of them, but I cautioned myself mightily against over indulgence and reached for an apple instead.

Who knows, I'll probably die of an insecticidal spray which annually taints the apple crop, when I could have just eaten another egg and taken my chances.

After all, it's Easter and time to celebrate.

Longing for Her Chest

I approached the back door, and there they were.

Beautiful works of art, basking in the sun.

They were porcelain white and flawless.

I was in awe.

"How do you do it?" I asked my friend.

Is she a painter? You might ask.

A sculptor? You might wonder.

No, she owns the prettiest ice chests I've ever seen, outside of a store.

"Ours are only this white on the day they're purchased," I admitted, and she was almost embarrassed for me.

"Well, we've had some incidents, so now the rule is that the ice chests are washed and bleached first, and left to dry, no exceptions."

I admire a house with rules. I have rules, too, but they are usually just laying around broken like the ice chests.

I returned to the office with a ghost-like appearance.

"You're not going to believe what I saw in their garage," I said to the husband, and he moved closer to hear my revelation. He surely suspected me to report finding a dead body, given my ashen appearance. He listened attentively, wondering what dirt I had dug up on this family, when I was actually sharing cleanliness, which is of course, next to godliness.

I told him how the ice chests stood at attention. How they glistened in the sun. How you could eat a salad out of them, or even bathe in them.

"Who would want to do that?" he asked.

"That's not the point," I said, keeper of broken rules. "It's just that you could."

"They probably don't catch as many fish as we do," he said in our defense.

"She had a 32-inch grouper—the boat record," I countered.

"Well, they have more time to clean than we do," he said.

And we both knew it wasn't so.

"So why can't we have clean ice chests?" I asked, like a child wondering why we can't own a home in Aspen.

"Our ice chests are clean," he maintained. "They just don't look like it."

I've got to remember that disclaimer the next time unexpected company drops by. "Oh, our house is clean—it just doesn't look like it."

I hate to resort to envy, but I went home and looked at our ice chests longingly. We clearly don't measure up. If I had been driving the truck that day, I would have loaded up four of them and driven to the dump.

I found the red one loitering out by the pump house, having held bait too long. I'm not sure anything short of a nuclear bomb will rid the chest of its aroma.

Another red one had been used to wash the new puppy, back when she fit. It was airing out in a different direction.

The third one is a small cooler, and I opened it cautiously as I've learned to do after 25 years of marriage (and fish). I took a deep breath and prepared myself for anything. I've encountered some unforgivable sights and smells in the past but on this day, all I found inside it was a wire basket of crickets gasping for breath.

The next ice chest—and my personal favorite—held the ingredients for the gasoline mix required for the gas-powered scooter. It had been transformed into a short work table, so that the necessary components were at hands' reach. It's clean on the inside, but you've got to clean off the top to get to the inside—that would include a funnel, a container of oil, a gas can, a measuring cup, and an abstract stain made by the repetition of that process.

"We are hopeless," I realized, as I looked at the menagerie of treasures which has landed in our garage: salvaged military items, tools which beg to be used, bicycles in various stages of disrepair, and shoes which have been helped to the garbage can by the puppy who smiled at me from the cast net upon which she was resting as she chewed on a Mountain Dew can.

That's when I saw it: the fifth and final cooler in our war chest.

It was actually clean, and I surveyed it carefully. I think it's large enough for my funeral when that day comes. I just hope they don't forget about me in the garage.

A Remote Kingdom

The husband was away for the evening, in search of a big fish.

After the children were nestled all snug in their beds, I limped down the stairs where my eyes fell upon the television remote control device on the end table.

Should I?

Could I?

The remote, you see, (by the process of eminent domain) has become the husband's property. I realize he has no legal right to it, but I rarely fight for television time and am generally content to watch 10 minutes of whatever is showing before I resume my routine. Therefore, I have spent little quality time with the remote.

It hardly knows my name.

But there it sat, staring at me, and pointing nervously at the television set.

Would she?

Could she?

I looked to my left and then to my right; there was no one in the room to object. So I picked up the control and instantly felt a surge of power through my being.

"This is my castle," I heard myself say and, even I found the phrase curious.

I plopped on the couch, as I have observed genuine remote controllers do. I began channel surfing, refusing to stay very long on the husband's favorites. Oh, there's the Weather Channel. I don't care if it rains or shines. Oooh, here's CNN 1,2, and 14, and I don't care. Jimmy Crack Corn, and I don't care … my master's gone away.

I paused on channels he would never tolerate; it was sheer wife rebellion. I watched a little shopping which even I—a shopper—can't understand. Then I flipped to a little home renovation. A little art. A little symphony music just to annoy no one.

Then I made a declaration of independence for the evening: there would be no John Wayne movies in this house tonight. No westerns. No wars. No pestilence. No legislation. No documentaries on Tecumseh.

Tonight, I was going to watch mindless t.v. without any guilt or ridicule.

Finding mindless t.v. programs isn't a difficult task. Deciding which one to land upon is, but I waded through all the major networks, all the movie stations and finally picked one I shall not disclose.

No one will ever know.

Because I was home alone.

With the remote.

I used the "mute" button at will, laughing all the while. Then I rearranged the time setting just for the fun of it; he will want to know if the power went off. I will be cool.

I learned how to operate "Go To" and managed to watch two mindless programs at one time, which is spring practice for football season.

I even ate cookies while lying on the couch, holding the remote. I tried to drink milk in that position but I was no good at it. I started to throw my socks on the floor, but I knew I'd have to pick them up.

Even so, it was paradise on earth.

If it hadn't been for the specter of rising early to get the daughter to school, I might have stayed up all night just to see what it really feels like to go to sleep with that remote in your hand. Still in control. Still pushing the buttons, as your head falls off the arm rest. Forty-nine times. Before you realize it's 2 a.m. and time for bed.

Yes, I was king for the night.

And master of the universal remote.

Shell Shocked

The temperature was eyeing 100 degrees and the lines through U.S. Customs were as long as the building which housed them, but we had plenty of time before boarding our 3 p.m. plane which would take us from Nassau, Bahamas, to Atlanta, Ga., and then to Tallahassee, Fla.

We had no fruit to declare, no animals, no foreign soil. We had placed our manicure scissors inside the luggage we would check, according to the rules of flight since the horrors of 9/11.

We each had a suitcase, although the ownership of items from one to the other had been blurred in the fury of packing to return home. All the wet bathingsuits had been added to the son's suitcase because he had nothing but dirty clothes anyway.

The husband's binoculars, which he added to his suitcase as an afterthought, ended up in mine when the souvenirs took up more space than we had planned.

Our birth certificates were certified and had raised, official stamps. We had photo i.d.'s and boarding passes.

An airport worker shuttled the daughter's suitcase onto the conveyor belt for outgoing Delta flights, and then motioned for the other three of us to step aside for a random search. I think we look suspiciously normal.

I rolled my eyes, realizing I'm always happy for them to search someone else, but not too happy to be the subject of the hunt. "Is this book about a dog?" the female officer asked the son, and he said "Yes, ma'am." She pushed his luggage aside. The husband had our large suitcase which workers rifled through with very little regard for my ingenious packing methods. "You can step aside," said the woman with the British accent.

Since I look like I teach Sunday School, I expected her to wave me on through, but she sniffed my shampoo bottle, sifted through all my underwear and opened the binocular case.

Out fell a 20-gauge shotgun shell.

Down fell my 20-gauge heart.

"What is this?" asked the short, dark-skinned woman who had eyes like Cruella deVille.

I was careful not to use the word "gun."

"It's a shell," I said, and she looked annoyed that I might be toying with her because it obviously wasn't like any shell you'd find on a beach in her country.

"What's it for?" she asked again.

"It goes in a … gun," I said, trying to be pleasant and forthcoming, although all I could picture was the prison we had toured in the old fort at the top of the hill.

"What's it doing in there?" I asked the husband with daggers in my eyes.

"What's it doing in there?" he said, repeating the question to the son who owns a 20-gauge shotgun.

"Uh, that's mine," said the son, in his truest Taylor County, Fla., accent. "We use those binoculars hunting and that's the last time I had them; I probably just dropped a shell in there. It's my fault."

She didn't care.

"We don't have the gun which shoots this shell," I explained to the woman who had obviously never seen such ammunition. "So it can do no one harm," I explained. "It was just a mistake—I had no idea it was in the case."

"Sit right here," she said, motioning me to the side. "I've got to call an LEO."

"What's an LEO?" I asked, wondering if I should just open the shell, ingest its contents and light a match.

"A law enforcement officer," she said.

It's a wonder that shell didn't explode by means of spontaneous combustion, for I was having a hot flash that would rival all others.

The daughter—worried about me, worried about the boys, worried about our future, or whether we had one—held up one side of the building while the husband and son tried to be cooperative. I was sitting, as I had been told, and thinking bad thoughts.

I had personally packed every item in three of the suitcases—except for those binoculars.

For the next 20 minutes of my life, there was a parade of officers in British regalia—examining the shell. I think they would have been happier if it had been cocaine or something they recognized.

When the LEO arrived, I did the dishonorable thing and pointed directly at the husband. "The binoculars are his," said I.

Then I decided to look casual, and I painted my fingernails while I sat with the lady officials and exchanged niceties. I eyed the clock: 45 minutes to take-off.

"It's fine, I'm sure," said one, probably wishing she had been the examiner to find the shotgun shell. I believe she would have thrown it in the trash and moved on.

While I sat, the husband answered 500 questions, showed his hunting license, his Kiwanis membership, his movie rental card, gave out his Social Security number, his driver's license number and promised never, oh never, to travel with a 20-gauge shotgun shell for the rest of his natural life. I couldn't help but think that in Taylor County, you could go to Christmas Eve Mass with a shotgun shell in your pocket and nobody would drop a candle.

"I'm sorry," said the son, to one of the officers-in-charge. "It's mine. I didn't know it was in there, and I didn't know he was bringing the binoculars." He, too, remembered that jail in the fort at the top of the hill.

Finally, the biggest, baddest Customs officer in the whole Commonwealth of the Bahamas showed up with braided cords on his sleeves and official badges all over his shirt. I feared the worst.

He was quiet as he rolled the shell in his fingers. He looked at it intently and said, "Hmm, you won't blow much away with this."

He took the shell, released the husband, patted the boy, loaded my luggage and bid me adieu. Don't worry, be happy.

Without CPR, I began breathing on my own again. I even began talking to my family and liking them (however slightly) again.

I did not, however, want to laugh about it then.

I do not want to laugh about it now.

But I may be able to laugh about it tomorrow, mon. We be jamming then.

*Little
Phone
on the Prairie*

I Liked Phones Better When They Were at the End of the Hall

When I was growing up, the telephone was located at the end of the hall in our three-bedroom, red brick house which had white shutters.

That was the phone's location not just in my house, but in everybody's house. The telephone sat at the end of the hall, in a special little nook which was created just for it.

You didn't have to ask, "Where's the phone?"

You didn't have to wonder, "How do you use it?"

You simply walked down the hall and there it was. You picked up the receiver if you were interested.

It seems that carpenters in the 1950s were only allowed certain privileges for creativity. They could have fun woodworking fireplace mantels, kitchen cabinets and the nook-at-the-end-of-the-hall which served as a shrine to the phone. After all, this wasn't Rome or Greece we were building; it was a small dwelling for a neighborhood of other small dwellings. No one was trying to land on the cover of House Beautiful; our friends and neighbors were just looking for a roof and some closet space.

In that era, the placement for the phone also defined its importance. It wasn't located in the kitchen, or in the family room, but at the end of the hall. In other words, you weren't to watch t.v. while talking on the phone, or while eating. If you had a phone call, you walked toward the phone which was invariably black. It didn't look like a football or a television remote; it looked like a phone.

The cord of this telephone could reach exactly 12 inches. Everyone you talked with and everything you said was open for public scrutiny, or worse: parental scrutiny. The end of my hall wasn't very far from the den, thus those sitting around the fireplace could choose to read the newspaper or listen to my phone conversation.

If we had been liberated young adults, we would have fought for our rights, but we were just glad our parents owned a house and bought a phone. We weren't about to argue about its color, or our access. We weren't that stupid.

Recently, I was in a phone store in our community, and to re-state the obvious, phones are clearly the newest fashion statement. You can buy covers so that your phone matches your car, matches your shoes, or matches your hair. It leaves me bewildered and remembering Barbie. She's about the only thing I ever wanted to buy accessories for, except for myself, of course.

I do, however, recall desperately wanting a Princess phone. I asked for it two Christmases in a row. By this time, phones came in designs other than black. There was a slimline and a Princess. Several of my friends—who were clearly less deserving—had been bequeathed with the Princess model. It was like buying your way into royalty.

My crown, however, never came down the chimney.

I continued to use our black phone at the end of the hall, always watching what I said to whom. As a compromise, the parents eventually bought a cord that was 24 inches long and I could pull the telephone into my bedroom and shut the door while I talked. It was as close as I ever got to being a Princess.

Members of today's generation would clearly perish if they did not have phones to carry with them everywhere they go. These phones serve as alarm clocks, cameras, calculators and personal secretaries while providing access to e-mail/Internet services for college students who talk to everybody they know, every hour.

Not wanting "to put all my eggs in one basket," I caution against too much dependence on an object called a telephone. "What if you lose it?" I ask with fear in my eyes, for it reminds me of the control lever on automobiles which monitors cruise control, the lights, wipers and your blood sugar level. If it breaks, you must park the car and hyperventilate.

Besides, I've used the phone enough at work by 5 p.m. to take a well-deserved vacation from it until the next morning. I don't need games and songs, call forwarding or waiting, speed calling, reminders to check the time, or Beethoven's Fifth in bell tones. Just a plain old ring, like the one the fire station sounds for emergencies.

And don't call me on your phone from the bathroom. I will hang up.

Clearly, I was never cut out to be, or to own, a Princess.

Life is Good, Around a Tomato Sandwich

When I was a child, I understood as a child: that is, I didn't fully appreciate what grew outside our kitchen door.

I respected, although never completely understood, my father's love for his cultivated pears and plums, his green apples and tomatoes on the vine.

I took those freshly shelled peas for granted, and assumed that just-baked cornbread was always on a table. Apple tarts? They would always be there, too, wouldn't they?

When I put away childish things, I came to realize that home-grown vegetables and fruits are among God's finest gifts to us.

So are those who grow them.

And those who cook them … the right way.

Early one summer, when the heat was beginning to make its fury known, I became the recipient of a bag of tomatoes which made me miss my father terribly.

They were grown by the kitchen door and each had reached the size of a small canteloupe.

Further, they tasted like a tomato was meant to taste. It was love at first sight.

How many slices of a real tomato does it take to make a sandwich in the South?

One.

Yes, these tomatoes were wide enough to cover a slice of white bread and lean off the sides a bit.

Add mayonnaise.

Add salt and pepper.

Fix yourself a glass of tea with a slice of lemon and be glad that you are living on this day in history.

For life is good, around a tomato sandwich like that.

As long as my gift bag of tomatoes supplied our dietary needs, I turned up my nose at the display of vegetables which the store called "tomatoes."

For they are not.

They are impostors from Venezuela. Or Mexico. But they have never seen black dirt, and wouldn't have a clue about what to do on a piece of white bread.

Now that my bag of gift tomatoes is depleted, I can't snub those in the grocery store.

"Maybe this one's okay," I say to myself as I place it in a plastic bag.

Yeah, it's okay, but it's only okay … and it's not the tomato's fault. You've got to love the earth in order to grow good tomatoes, and it's that love of the earth which gives the tomato its distinct, satisfying flavor.

I am sure.

With such a keen appreciation for the vegetable, it is certainly regrettable that there are no vegetable gardeners at my house. What we lack in talent, we make up for in enthusiasm.

Each year, we purchase several tomato plants. They're so lovable: six inches high, perfectly green and healthy, with yellow blooms on their small branches.

We take them home and plant them. We water them. We fertilize them. We notice they're not as green as they once were. We wonder why. We spray them. We dust them.

Then we get our annual allowance of three tomatoes (per plant) and the entire vine turns yellow and shrivels up in protest … but refuses to die. Instead, it stands there with three green leaves at the top, as a reminder of our own inadequacy and our dependence upon individuals who can keep vines green and harvest tomatoes-upon-tomatoes, for weeks upon weeks.

This is a salute to those individuals who toil in the heat and battle Mother Nature, for the fruit of the vine.

Next year, we're going to bring our three plants to your house, right outside your kitchen door where all things green and wonderful grow.

To pay homage.
And to have a tomato sandwich.

Little Phone on the Prairie

There was family news to share one Sunday afternoon, and it happened this way.

I called on the previous night with the initial Jr. Miss pageant news, but we did not speak at length with Alabama relatives until the following day.

"Can you hear me?" asked my mother on the other end of the phone, as if she was talking through a tin can with a piece of string coming out of it.

"Yes, I can hear you," I said.

"Can you hear me?" I asked back.

"Yes," she said. "But this phone is so small, I can't believe it works."

"Whose phone are you talking on?" I asked.

"Your cousin's," she said. "He has unlimited weekend minutes."

I started laughing at that point. Poor cousin-of-mine; he's trying to educate the aunties on phone use in the new century.

"Here," she said, "talk to him."

We exchanged niceties, and spoke on how Scottish blood runs deep in this family. "They could each afford to own a phone company and they wait, instead, until you show up with unlimited minutes," I said.

"Yes," he chuckled politely. "Following instructions," he said, "I'm going to pass the phone around."

"Oh no," said I.

"Oh yes," said he, and I could envision his smile.

"What color was her dress?" asked the first aunt.

In fashion editor style, I tried to compose a succinct sentence of description, which started this way. "It was ice blue," but that was as far as I got, for she interrupted me to repeat that phrase to everyone at the table.

"It was ice blue," she said in announcement fashion.

My mother took the phone.

"How was her hair?" she asked.

I told her; she repeated it for the family circle.

"Mother, I can't do this," I said. "I'll just talk to you and you can report to them."

"I won't remember everything," she lamented.

"Did she win any scholarship money?" an aunt shouted over her, and I could hear the phone-owner, probably doubled over in laughter.

"Just let me tell the story to each of them," I said, and I took turns describing minute details to each family member, while inquiring about the health of each and asking about the cousins.

"Anything else?" my mother asked at the conclusion of this ritual which was worse than any judge's interview.

"We're going to give you back to your cousin because we don't know how to shut this thing off," she said without even a goodbye.

"This is like Little House on the Prairie gets a phone," I said to the phone and its owner.

"It's worse," he agreed.

"I gave them pre-paid calling cards, but you mother said hers didn't work. After I educated them on how to use the cards, I realized your mother still has a rotary phone, so she has to go to her sister's house to use the card," he said, chuckling.

Actually, my mother doesn't have *just any* rotary phone. She has the one Noah used when he called land. Circa 1950, the phone's receiver could render any prowler unconscious because of its sheer weight. We keep it for both sentiment and protection.

Since this cousin recently resided in Dallas, Texas, where he retired from a large international accounting firm, returning to Sweet Home Alabama has been a treat. Especially when you return to the uttermost parts where Unlimited Minutes on a Weekend call for a family reunion to see how serious these phone companies are about their offer.

"We've got to go," he said. "We've got other people to call. We're not going to leave a stone unturned. We're going to think about all 50 states and see if we can find a person in each," he said, as the aunts adored him from a distance and giggled in tribute.

"I'm pleased to represent Florida," I said. "And if AT&T arrests you for exploiting Unlimited Minutes, please use your last dime to call me," I encouraged.

"It's 50 cents now, Susan," he said, and he was right. This time the aunts laughed at me and shouted "Goodbye" in unison.

It was a Sunday smile I won't soon forget.

A Colony of Aunts

I love my aunts. My two favorite aunts, along with my mother, comprise the trio which my brother-in-law affectionately calls, "The Little Women." When he refers to this trio, he uses a hand motion that is nothing but a sweeping flat line extending from one arm to the other.

That's his way of explaining that the aunts, and the mother, are virtually the same height; they could be triplets but the youngest would surely protest about being called the same age as the older, and the middle wouldn't enjoy being assumed the oldest. They are "doorsteps," they will tell you, with two years separating each. The baby will be 80 in a few weeks. You do the math.

They have gray hair and a spry gait. They carry pocketbooks and have cute shoes (one wears a size 4). They laugh a lot, fight a little, and maintain that both are okay. Nobody in my family challenges them. Nobody in their right mind challenges them.

I don't want to rush old age, but I don't fear it either, and I have my mother and my aunts to thank for that. They make 80 look like 40 with an attitude. Oh sure, health issues have arisen in the last 20 years that nobody welcomed: a couple of heart bypasses, breast cancer, arthritis. But they take two aspirin, fuss with their doctors, get out and walk.

They have buried their husbands and learned to carve new lives out of what was left. They have thrown new paint on the walls and on their fingernails.

They have coffee on Monday afternoons, rotating hostess duties with 8-10 close friends. They have circle meetings throughout the week, and gather on Sue's deck in the afternoons to watch the golfers on the local course. On Fridays, they may go out for lunch, or drive to Alabama's capital city where there are countless opportunities for eating and shopping.

They don't miss a wedding, a birthday party, a town meeting or a good sale. They visit the Golden Isles of Georgia, travel by bus to Branson, Mo., and go to the beach (if but only to look at it). They recently drove to Dallas, Texas, but that's when they were only 78, 76 and 74.

Although we don't speak of their demise, when *they* do, it's in practical terms: "We just hope one of us can speak, one of us can hear, and one of us can see. We want you to put us in the same room in the nursing home and come to see us when you can." That's the message to the four children and eight grandchildren who gather around their tables, in a rotation which acknowledges holidays and celebrations.

And there is little distinction between the tables—one is almost as much like home, as the other.

Recently, for my mother's 84th birthday, her friends made grand plans while she looked at me dead-in-the-eye and said, "I can't believe I'm this old." Her friends include, of course, the two aunts and, on this occasion, three school buddies. They went through 12 years of school together and still hang out, at 84.

These friends determined that they would visit the new art museum affiliated with Auburn University, and then enjoy lunch together before returning home by way of the mall to see if there was a good sale.

Because of the goodness of Divine Providence, the daughter's class schedule at Auburn University changed at the last minute and she was able to join them for this event. She called the night before to alert the grandmother and what a gift it was. "Hazel has a cell phone," my mother noted, telling the granddaughter to expect their call when they were heading to lunch.

"Take your cell phone," mother said to her middle sister, who was eager to comply.

I didn't ask, but they probably left home at the crack of dawn, only to be disappointed that the museum didn't open at 7:30 a.m. Nonetheless, their lives were culturally enhanced by this visit and they worked up a good appetite, too.

The rest of the story unfolded as the daughter shared lunch with them.

The grandmother took the floor, at the table. "Well, when we got ready to call you, I told Hazel to get out her phone and dial your number. And guess what she pulled from her purse?"

"What?" the granddaughter said, almost afraid to ask.

"The television remote. She brought the television remote instead of her cell phone." As exhibit A, the middle sister produced the television remote from her cute purse, with a sheepish look on her face.

The Little Women laughed. The granddaughter laughed. They laughed and laughed. If you laugh, your arthritis doesn't hurt so much.

When the aunt's birthday lands, I hope I have the opportunity to tell her and the other Little Women how wonderfully they have influenced my past and how confidently they pave the way to the future.

I plan to call and convey those sentiments.

If, that is, I can find my remote.

Our Hearts Belonged to Seymour

There Bettylin and I stood in flip-flops and faded denim shorts 'neath the old apple tree.

Paying our last respects.

We were grieving for a turtle named Seymour. He had served us well. He had been our friend. Our slow but sure nature study. Our link to the watery world.

We loved Seymour.

But one day …

Life comes to an end, and suddenly people remember us fondly. (It's a shame to have to die in order to be well-liked.)

Seymour attained new popularity through his death.

Although Bettylin and I were the only ones who had much to do "with that stupid old turtle" (which was the unkind label attached by insensitive boys in the neighborhood), when a funeral was planned, everybody wanted to attend.

"You never even liked him," said Bettylin in her loud and hateful voice, with one hand upon her hip as her toe tapped out frustration.

"Yeah," I said, always being the original sort.

"You called him, 'stupid old turtle,'" said Bettylin with turtle tears welling in her own eyes.

"Yeah," I said.

"And you," she said, bringing her discourse to a crescendo, "you once tried to kill him. Who knows, you might have killed him this time."

"Yeah," I said, looking at her curiously. Had grief affected her mental processes? Seymour died a natural death in his plastic circular home with the pool.

I knew it, and she knew it.

"We didn't kill that stupid old turtle," Sidney insisted. "He probably died of being stupid."

"That's it," said Bettylin, grabbing the closest clod of red dirt that she could find.

"Yeah," I said.

After she returned from dirt-bombing our arch enemy, I held this bereaved human mother's hand and told her just to ignore those boys figuring they'd probably die of being stupid soon, too.

We had funeral arrangements to make, and they were elaborate.

For Seymour, as for no other, Bettylin would part with the red plastic heart she got on Valentine's Day—the kind that comes filled with conversation hearts. Seymour would rest in peace within that plastic symbol of friendship, knowing that his survivors enshrouded him with love.

"What about music?" I asked. This was, of course, my first funeral.

We sang "Jesus Loves Me" to Seymour 'neath the old apple tree. God's greatest melodies find new meaning when sung from the heart.

That day, we sung from our hearts.

Then we surrounded Seymour's little green shell with cotton from the aspirin bottles at our two houses. And we buried that red Valentine heart.

We made a small commemorative cross from two popsicle sticks (which compelled us to first eat the popsicles), held together by a bit of Elmer's school glue. We wrote upon them: "Seymour, a good turtle," and the date, June 12, 1963.

At the most solemn moment of the ceremony, Sidney and his neighborhood partner-in-crime, charged from behind the hedge with primitive guns made from limbs. "Seymour's dead, and you two are next," they bellowed.

"At a funeral!" I said in disgust, already being the keeper of morals.

"We're telling," was the final word as Seymour's funeral entourage marched through the poplar trees, around the mimosas and through the fragrant sweet shrub to the back screened door.

For what must have been the 17th time that day, we announced, "Those boys are aggravatin' us again.'"

"Uh huh," my mother said, while grating corn. "Just ignore them."

We felt obligated to lick our wounds, mourn Seymour's passing and our own misfortune of being left on this earth with those boys.

It's a misfortune which we continued to lament in the course of our growing up, until we wore chiffon at each other's wedding.

But we never lamented our times with Seymour. He was as meaningful in life as he was inspirational in death.

"Seymour, a good turtle."

Our hearts (and the plastic one, too) belonged to him.

Going Home Again

They say you can't go home again, but you really should try.

That may sound like an easy endorsement to you, but it's not. Translation: it's worth staying up until midnight the night before doing laundry; it's worth packing at 6:30 a.m.; it's worth working six hours and then traveling another six with two children who'd rather be doing almost anything … except riding in a car.

"This could be our last trip to Alabama," I announced in desperation to the children who had imaginatively divided the back seat into two portions and were fighting about whose legs were in violation. It's hard to play "I Spy," count cows or draw in the dark at 65 m.p.h.

When we pulled into the first driveway I ever learned to pull into, all the laundry, packing, fighting and fuming seemed worthwhile.

In the dark of the night, there was a porch light burning. The garage was illuminated. All the neighbors had to know I was coming home.

I threw the grandchildren toward their waiting grandmother and handed each a bag to carry in.

Within the first hour, the grandmother had reviewed all the births, deaths and divorces since Christmas, over onion dip and chips. She poured soft drinks and soft praise for the children. She handed each of us a napkin and reminded us to use it. The children had to understand from whence I came, and from whence they came.

The bathtub there is slicker than today's fiberglass versions. The children practice their breast stroke while there. The water is softer.

The quilts on the bed are thicker. The lights are dimmer. The phone rings louder.

When you're 40, you start making those comparisons.

Night comes easier there; the neighborhood is quieter and the phone doesn't ring after dark. There's not much to do past 9 p.m., and so the children agree to sleep.

And we delight in their opportunity to sleep, then ours.

Sleep is a luxury of going home again.

Of course, morning comes quickly and I smell sausage.

There are only 24 hours left for visiting. The suitcase is turned upside down as four people dress at four different times. The husband needs a haircut; the cake must be picked up for lunch; the five-year-old needs a playmate, and we all take turns.

Then we pile in the car to see the aunts. "Boy, they live close," said the son who feels that all cousins must be six hours away at 65 m.p.h. Actually the aunts are only blocks away and they obediently drag out old toys for the little one to play with, while we catch up on kith and kin. We see the latest pictures from their respective grandchildren and find out what's happening at the nursing home.

It's off to the other aunt's home where nobody answers the door. Not to worry; it's not locked. So I go in, speaking the traditional ... "Aunt Hazel, yoo-hoo," greeting and she does not worry.

She's asleep on the sofa in her bedroom, with the remote in hand. She wakes up and begins talking immediately; she doesn't need coffee, water or space, just an audience. I've never seen anybody wake up and deliver a soliloquy with such ease.

Within minutes, we're in her car and she's showing us all the new homes in the area. "That roof just doesn't match the house and I don't know why they picked it. Do you?"

Even the children were nodding in common agreement on the roof. It was all so curious.

We later found playmates with baseball gloves, some antiques to paw over and a baby gift, before we returned where the husband was manning the grill in the backyard and throwing the football to new friends.

Yes, the neighbors have buried husbands and wives. The children are, for the most part, gone. But they come home again, even though someone once said you couldn't. And they find themselves retrieving frisbees off the roof with a ladder, chatting with neighbors who have aged and know you have too.

Home has an enduring way of always luring you back, and tucking you in amongst generations of quilts.

Leaving the porch light on.

And embracing new generations with the amenities which distinguish it from any other place, and make it sweet.

'Tis
The
Season
To Be Jolly

'Twas the Night Before the Water Pump Was Fixed

I had just settled in for a long day of laundry, when in the washing machine, there arose such a clatter that I sprang from the kitchen to see what was the matter.

The water, which previously flowed from the machine with ease, now spurted and spewed while I pleaded, "Oh no, please … oh no, please …"

Then suddenly amidst all the clatter, the water—it stopped. I couldn't have felt badder (worse).

Away to the window, I flew like a flash. Tore open the shutters and threw up the sash. The dog slept soundly as if nothing was wrong; the boy was shooting hoops and singing a song.

I looked for puddles of water around our abode. Had the dog left the hose on and drained our well dry? Or was it the boy? The husband? Oh my, oh my.

I walked around the house where the stockings were hung by the chimney with care. I enlisted the son's help, hoping he would worry about how I might fare.

"Does this mean I don't have to take a bath?" he asked.

What to my wondering eyes should appear but a vision of the husband, out hunting eight tiny reindeer. I reached for the phone, so lively and quick, called his hunting companion and felt rather sick.

Yes I was sad and apologetic, too, but there's no water at this house and I don't know what to do.

I envisioned the husband traveling my way, with a sleigh full of toys and St. Nicholas at bay. Instead, his voice came through the phone waves with a bound, and he gave me tests to enact on the grounds. "We can't fix it," he finally said. "We've hit a brick wall. All that's left is to make the call."

As dry leaves that before the wild hurricane fly, when they meet with an obstacle mount to the sky, I scurried through our backyard, frantic and frenzied, hoping the pump repairman would soon be there.

And then, in a twinkling, I heard in the fog, the barking and pawing of our old watchdog. As I drew in my head and was turning around, down the driveway he came with a bound. He wasn't dressed all in fur, from his head to his toe. He wore jeans and boots, and shared my woe. A bundle of tools he had flung on his back, and he looked like a peddler, just opening his pack. His eyes, how they twinkled as he approached the pump's stall and then he said, "I'm glad you called."

Suddenly, my cheeks were like roses and my complexion was white as snow. I don't want a pump for Christmas, this I know. But a wink of his eye and a twist of his head soon gave me to know I had nothing to dread.

Until, that is, he said the motor on the pump was gone and the pump—too—would soon be dead.

How I wished I was nestled all snug in my bed, with visions of sugar-plums dancing in my head.

But no, I was in the pump house with a flashlight and a friend, hoping no creatures would be stirring for I'm afraid of both mice and repairmen.

"No water tonight," he said, but he told me not to fear. He filled not the stockings but jugs with water that was clear, and reminded me thoughtfully that the neighbors were near.

"Just give me 12 hours," he said, "and you'll have water again."

'Twas the night before the water pump was fixed that we bathed in a bowl, gave thanks for the heat, and made running water our new goal.

The Twelve Hours of Christmas passed in relative calm as our water system took a paid vacation, but meant us no harm. It's early in December, and two visits from the Jolly Old Man have already been recorded. He returned the next day, spoke not a word and went straight to his work. The water it ran, down the hoses and up the pipes. When he had finished, he did not lurk.

He sprang to his sleigh, to his wife gave a whistle, and away they all flew like the down of a thistle.

And I heard him exclaim ere he drove out of sight, "Merry Christmas to all, and to all … water! Tonight."

Even Wise Men Lose Their Heads

Annually, we deliver the nativity scene from the attic and place the ceramic animals and figures upon our piano so that we can adore them for the month of December.

The nativity scene was a wedding gift, 25 years ago, from a bridesmaid who made every figure with her own two hands and bundled them in newspaper for safe-keeping (and to underscore our chosen profession).

"Carefully," I said to the son as I explained how the pieces were, virtually, irreplaceable. He slowed down to satisfy me, turned to place a donkey, and dropped a wise man … right upon his wise head, on the ceramic tile floor.

He screamed; I screamed; everybody screamed.

The daughter studied us cautiously to see this drama unfold. It was one of those moments when I wanted to abandon all I know to be right and good, and instead to shout, scream and curse—at the child and at the world.

But, apparently what I know to be right and good had a better hold on me on this day, and all I could do was sit there and grieve, picking up the pieces of the wise man's ceramic turban.

The son was horrified, volunteered to leave home and find another family because he was too stupid for this one. I listened but said nothing as I considered what to do next. When I could finally breathe and think, I gathered my wits among the pieces of a wise man's turban.

"I think it's going to be fine," I said to the son, as he was running upstairs to gather his worldly belongings. I sat in the floor and further assessed the damage. Thanks to the God of Christmas, I was confident the wise man would be whole again. So I ran upstairs too, stopped all the packing and showed the son the wise man. He was just temporarily decapitated, I explained. It was a clean break around his neck—I could fix that easily. The three sections of turban came back together to form a kingly look, and I was confident the procedure could be accomplished with ceramic glue and minimized with touch-up paint.

"He just has a headache," I told the son, "but he probably did the night he followed the star, too."

We decided to keep our family together for yet another Christmas and I think I saw the wise man smile, but it was hard to tell if it was a grimace or a smile.

"Your sister once broke Baby Jesus' toe," I told the son, as we finished the set-up.

"I did not," she said, "he did that too."

"I did not," he said.

"You broke the toe, didn't you?" I asked the sister.

"No, it was him. He dragged that Baby Jesus all around the house when he was a baby. Don't you remember?"

This is what happens when history falls prey to revisionists, and even though I'm taking a soy supplement, I'm not sure I can trust my memory either. So if somebody breaks Baby Jesus' toe, you really should write it down or you'll be accusing the wrong person one day.

"Anyway," I said, "it doesn't matter. The baby is fine; the toe is fine; the wise man's head will be fine by tomorrow."

"I heard there weren't really three wise men," said the daughter.

"Go away," said the son.

"Well, it's irrelevant," I said confidently. "It doesn't matter how many there were. Paul Harvey says Rutgers University is studying the plant from which myrrh comes and it's been found to kill cancer cells in laboratory tests," I reported.

"No way," said the daughter.

"There's a lot more to a nativity scene than meets the eye," I concluded. The children scattered, and left the whole lot of animals and biblical characters on top of the piano to keep watch upon the house.

I like having them around at Christmas, thinking about the hay and straw, and the star which shone so brightly. I even like the broken baby toe, and the tri-sectioned, wise-man turban for it makes me confident that—like the Velveteen Rabbit—these characters can be real.

If you let them.

Gifts Without Ribbons

I looked in the back seat as the car zoomed through the dark of the cold night and I said to myself, "These are not our children."

They looked like our children, the ones that have been with us for 16 and 9 years respectively. But they weren't acting like our children after three days on the road, too much sugar, and too little back seat.

"Could you hand me my CD player?" asked one.

The other one did so without complaining, and I heard a "thank you" emerge from the darkness.

I looked at the husband but he was focusing on yellow and white lines, traffic behind us and other traffic coming toward us.

I decided that if I stared at him, he would soon notice me and I could mouth the question, "Whose children do we have in the back seat?"

He never looked, and I don't do well at containing information I feel compelled to share. So I finally leaned over, trying not to attract the attention of the back seat and I said, "These are not our children in the back seat."

"What?" he asked in return.

I repeated my belief.

He smiled and looked in the rear view window: they were children off a television program, being kind to one another, equally sharing the back seat, quietly listening to music we didn't want to hear, on their earphones.

Forget my presents, this was the only gift I needed.

It was Christmas Eve and everybody else on the planet was where they meant to be. We, however, had been to both grandmothers' homes, and were returning to our own where a familiar pillow would be welcomed.

There were many gifts of the season which had no ribbons:

- everyone was healthy;

- most of the relatives were present and accounted for;

- the grandmothers said, "let them eat cake," and we did;

- Christmas music resounded from a little white church whose location on a peninsula gives it three reflections in the surrounding lake;

- there were cousins a'plenty with footballs and fishing poles;

- there were friends who become walking scrapbooks after decades of memories shared;

- there were American flags flying throughout the South;

- and manger scenes of every description;

- friends telephoned their holiday wishes;

- and sent a bumper-crop of Christmas cards, so that I ran out early in the season, just keeping up with the Joneses;

- we had heat and lights and food and shelter;

- we had gas for the car and safe travels;

And on top of all that, there were gifts under the tree which had ribbons.

In our Christmas prayers, we remembered the triumphs and horrors of the year past, and we gave thanks for all that is good in our collective lives.

For the gifts with ribbons.

And, especially for those without.

Silent Night

On our cross-country travels, I have left behind many essential items.
I've left behind toothbrushes and make-up.
I've traveled without jewelry and even extra underwear.
But never before have I forgotten something I missed so much.
On Christmas Day, 2003, however, we piled children, gifts and luggage into the Jeep and headed north.
Without my voice.
The timing was about as imperfect as timing can be. I saw people I haven't seen in a year, and won't see again, for another year. I had things to say, and listening is not my best gift. I tried to hang with the best of them, but it's hard to be witty and charming when you're doomed to silence.
As a compromise, I whispered to each and all. Those who know me best, mourned for me.
"You sound horrible," said one, wondering if I was contagious.
"You don't look like you feel good," said another, wondering if I was contagious.
"What have you brought us, that may kill us?" asked yet another, wondering if I was contagious.
I would have never taken a fever or the chills across the state line, but this symptom just seemed to be a symptom. It jumped in the car with the rest of us, and enjoyed looking out the window.
The curious thing about having laryngitis—or one of the curious things, anyway—is that people whisper back to you ... as if it's secrets, or something.

"You don't have to whisper back," I whispered to the daughter.

"Right," she said, whispering back.

The unfortunate side effect of the medical dilemma is that you can't easily issue commands. I looked the sister-in-law dead in the eye and said, "Would you please yell at the boys for me?"

But forcing myself to look on the bright side of this quiet Christmas, I had to admit that there are subtleties of family gatherings that you miss if you're talking.

I listened a whole lot more this Christmas ... to girl voices that are getting older and more confident, and to boy voices which (even at age 7) watch the Pittsburgh Steelers and declare before the adults think to, "Bad call. I'd challenge."

We played charades, ate turkey and ham, and oohed and ahhed over the cousin's new digital camera with its remote control which makes family portraits as directed from the back row of the picture.

We petted dogs and missed our own new puppy. We fished and hunted, slept late or not at all, visited aunts over the river and through the woods, and let them do the talking. They are immensely qualified.

We caught up with college roommates and rejoiced over good health for all. Laryngitis is, after all, just a diversion.

We swapped stories—old ones, new ones, true ones and those embellished. I love the stories of a family, regardless of the day or the holiday.

When we walked in the first back door, the grandmother said, "Merry Christmas and could you go get ice?"

Then she added, "How've you been, and could you change the bulb in the chandelier?"

And finally she wondered, "How's school, and could you butter the rolls?"

There were plenty of words to go around, even without mine.

After creating enough garbage to fill a landfill, we packed the sleigh again—with fishing rods on top—and bounded back through the woods to Real Time where the grocery store looms large and laundry always loyally waits for me.

But it's our life—every wonderful and awful moment of it, and we know we're fortunate to be given another year. For that we say thanks, Happy New Year to all, and glory be: my voice was right where I left it.

It stayed Home for the Holidays.

A Red Vest Christmas

Every year at Christmastime, I see red.

A red vest in the distance.

A red vest from the past.

My father was one of the most conservative dressers in the history of mankind. He wore a white shirt six days out of seven, always matched with a dark navy, deep brown or gray-black suit. His ties were painfully plain. Spit-shined shoes, socks he learned to darn in the U.S. Army, and a tie tack without any detailwork completed his attire.

Then one year, a bold family member gifted him a red vest for Christmas. It was the kind of red which I'm sure he associated with bawdy fingernail polish and indiscreet sections of large cities. He was polite, I am sure, but the whole family raised eyebrows as if to suggest, "Uncle Ed will never wear that."

Mother and I knew it to be true. The man, even with our prodding which he routinely ignored, would not leave the house in anything that red.

Out of the box, and on a clothes hanger the red vest went, where it rested for 12 months. No one talked about it. Few remembered its advent.

Until the Christmas Eve when my father emerged from his bedroom, wearing the red vest.

Mother and I were speechless. Our mouths dropped in unison. We looked at each other in complete disbelief and she finally found the courage to speak.

"Why Edddd," she said, "you look so nice in that vest."

He moved his pipe to the other side of his mouth and walked past us toward the car. It was our cue to shut up and follow.

"I like that red vest, Daddy," I said, bouncing in the back seat of the car.

It was a quiet car ride, but my mother smiled the whole way.

He was off to his in-laws' for Christmas Eve, and Lord knows, it was a gathering he enjoyed in short doses. For Mother's family was loud: they laughed a lot, they sang, they told jokes and played the piano. His family all wore black and went to the Baptist church for recreation.

When he stepped off the front porch, past the rocking chairs and into the living room which Grandmother had heated to a fare-thee-well, there was a large outcry from the relatives, as if they had converted the man. "Look at Ed's red vest," my aunt said.

"Uncle Ed?" his nephew asked incredulously, as if it might be an impostor.

"I can't believe you wore it," said another.

"That's enough," he said, motioning for a cessation of surprise. He found a chair in the corner from which he would observe the family's bustling in a scientific manner, smoking his pipe, wearing his red vest. I took a picture, but I was the only one who could get away with such silliness.

He later told me a story about his own father who served as sheriff of the Alabama county in which I grew up. He sounded straightforward, too, and given to little amusement. "But on Christmas Eve," my daddy told me, "he'd take his pistol out in the front yard and fire shots into the sky."

Years later, if I stare intently into the night sky at Christmas, I can hear shots fired in a front yard of long ago, and remember warmly a red vest which always bids me a Merry Christmas.

Fond of Fondue, Are You?

As I look back on the Christmas of 2003, I am confident that my family will forget all the perfect things I accomplished (for there are many), and they will recall the one night that I dreamed big.

And fell short.

In my quest to make the holidays especially meaningful for the one child who left our home in search of higher education, and the three of us who stayed behind, I picked days and nights out of the calendar during her time with us for special family events.

Not a marching band or anything, but a different dinner or a special outing to cause us to be congenial and kind.

Hope springs eternal in the human breast, you know.

I recalled how much we enjoyed a fondue dinner several years ago, and determined that with the Christmas china at four places, this would be an event to remember.

I got that part right.

Preparation for fondue only takes half your day, as you purchase the foods, wash and chop vegetables, cut meat into portions and prepare sauces. When I was finally ready for the family to assume their positions, I was exhausted ... but it's Christmas, I told myself, and everybody is exhausted.

I explained the rules, and I'm really good at that, although no one particularly enjoys it. Each family member was presented two color-coded forks and we were poised to proceed with dinner.

"Go," I said, and my family of four plunged meats and vegetables into batters and then hot grease which sounded as if it could consume the house.

That round went nicely, and we all got two bites of food. On the next round, the grease had cooled off, due to the small flame from a can a sterno, and wasn't cooking well at all.

"I'm hungry," said the youngest.

"I'm starving," said the eldest.

"This could take all night," said the husband.

Then they all felt badly for me, having gone to great lengths for two bites of food. Even with the Christmas china in place, it was hardly enough food to constitute a meal.

We put an alternate pot of cooking oil on the stove, and heated it to third-degree-burn level, then proceeded to interchange the grease, so that "sitting for dinner" took on new meaning. We were actually just passing each other on the way to the stove, or to the table.

It was the son, who doesn't care to tie his shoes or brush his teeth, who got us organized. "Give me the forks with meat," he said, "I'll work this pot. Now you work that one with the vegetables, and we'll use these plates to serve from."

We all looked at each other as if an angel had descended upon our fondue pot. Ouch.

The system worked pretty well—especially in light of the previous one, but it was the husband who drew my attention to the obvious pitfall.

"Do you realize," he asked, "that we have the youngest and least reliable member of the family leaning over a pot of hot grease while he balances on a bar stool?"

All the color drained out of my face which, to this point, had been flushed by the hot oil.

"But he's doing so well," I countered. Before Boy, I worried a great deal. Now I pretend I'm on valium and wait for the other shoe to fall.

"I think you could work at Mel's Diner," I said to the boy, since we're always finding careers for him.

"You could," said the sister. "Look at him."

He was actually singing as he poked forks in and out of batter, and then the grease. He had vegetables on one plate, meat on the other, and he was directing an imaginary orchestra with the "empty" forks.

I can't remember if we ate enough that night or not; I think we just stopped from sheer exhaustion. But it was certainly a night to remember.

That part, I got right.

Thou
Shalt
Not
Whine

Peck on Cheek Brings a Peck of Trouble

Andy Pinson lived dangerously when we were in kindergarten.

He was a sleek, lean, running machine who kissed girls.

And I was one of his victims.

While discussing this over dinner one night, my daddy told me to "run, run, run—as fast as you can. You don't want that nasty boy kissing you again."

So I ran, always away from Andy Pinson.

But he caught me on a number of occasions, right on the other side of one of the camellia bushes which grew lusciously in Mrs. Elvena Hamilton's backyard where our kindergarten met.

"Teacher, Andy Pinson kissed me again," I would tell in my loudest voice with my hands on my hips.

And Andy Pinson got in trouble. He was a repeat offender, you might say.

Or maybe for Andy, the crime was worth the punishment.

After 10 minutes in solitary, he'd be at it again: chasing all the five-year-old girls he saw, and kissing the ones he could catch. A bit more discreetly, however.

Even at 5, Andy was cool. He didn't just hang around with girls. The boys liked him, too. It wasn't that they necessarily approved of him kissing girls, but they gave him extra points for the aggravation factor and he earned them in an enthusiastic manner.

Soon, thereafter, Andy Pinson and his family moved. I never saw him or them again. I never even thought about him again.... until I read an

Associated Press article about a six-year-old boy in Lexington, N.C., who was suspended from school on the grounds of sexual harassment.

He kissed a girl in his class.

I looked quickly to see if his last name was Pinson; it was not.

Then I looked quickly to see if I was dreaming.

And then I slammed the newspaper on my desk in disgust (as many of you have probably done before).

Even contemplating a sexual harassment case against a kid who kissed a girl on the playground is ludicrous. I'm embarrassed for the school district in Lexington, N.C.

"But wait," I said to myself, trying to be objective. "Is he an unruly child with a history of lewd advances?"

The article listed no "priors" for this student, and suddenly, my intent gaze caught his picture: he's a blonde-headed kid with a bowl haircut, "Little Rascals" glasses and a smirky smile just like Andy Pinson.

It would seem to me that every school district in America has enough to do without punishing six-year-olds for being six-year-olds. He was sent to another room and disallowed to color, play or attend the ice cream party for students with good attendance.

If I had a law degree, I'd fly to Lexington and defend him.

I might even put myself on the stand. "Mrs. Lincoln, isn't it true that you were once victimized by a fellow kindergarten student?"

"Yes."

"What long-lasting side effects have you experienced from that incident?" a three-piece suit might ask me.

"Well," I would respond, with a Southern accent, "I have occasionally felt inclined to kiss men, especially around camellia bushes, and I have often wanted to find Andy Pinson—he was the perpetrator, you know. He's probably a preacher or something, maybe a judge, and I suspect that he's living a remarkably normal life, rearing children and paying taxes. Norman Rockwell would have been charmed by him, and by this little boy from Lexington, I am sure."

And, hey, when you've got Norman Rockwell on your side, there are no further questions and justice prevails.

Case dismissed.

Let's go buy crayons and ice cream for this young man and hope that America soon regains its sense of humor without feeling it has sacrificed any virture.

For it seems other virtues leave this country without so much as a passing glance.

And we're left to pick on six-year-olds who wear glasses.

Now that's harassment.

Choke the Motor, or Me?

As we pushed the husband out the door and toward the boat on Memorial Day, he said plaintively, "I don't know if we should be out on the Gulf of Mexico today; they're predicting thunderstorms, you know."

We looked to the heavens and saw sunshine.

We called Keaton Beach on the Taylor County coastline of Florida for a more accurate forecast.

We loaded the boat and headed south: the husband, the daughter and I. The son had staked his claim at this beach earlier in the weekend, and still declares that the most fun on earth begins there.

It's a quieter ride from town when it's just the three of us, and we were at the boat ramp when the husband actually realized that he didn't have a first mate.

"Okay," he said, looking at me like he was my football coach. "I want you to get in the truck and back the trailer straight down the ramp."

"Okay, coach," I said.

"I've got the truck and trailer lined up," he added. "Just go straight down the ramp," he emphasized with hand movements.

"Got it," I said, as the daughter stood on the sidelines, shaking her head and fearing the worst.

First, I had to adjust the seat in the truck because I'm vertically challenged. Then I had to adjust the rear view mirror, check my hair, and find the gear shift.

"Straight back," I said to myself as I began easing the boat and its trailer toward the water.

I am absolutely certain that I was going straight. But the trailer started veering toward the left, and then I tried to correct it with my steering, and the husband was motioning wildly for me to stop and try again.

He came to the window. Calmly, he explained again with more hand movements. "Straight down the ramp, easy as she goes."

After three tries, the coach pulled me.

"Maybe she can," I said, pointing to the daughter, fearing that she couldn't but wishing to share that distinction with somebody—anybody—else.

"Why don't you back the boat down the ramp and we'll get in the boat and crank it," the daughter suggested, trying role reversal.

"I'm not sure you can crank it," the husband said, having lost his confidence in his seaworthy vessel the previous weekend. "But whatever," he said, sensing defeat, and I knew he wished the weather had kept us home.

He backed that boat down the ramp as if he was born backing a boat down a ramp. I just sat there, re-playing my life's inadequacies while he made it look so simple.

"Okay," said the daughter, enjoying being in control. "Let's crank this boat and show him."

You know the noise: zuhn-a-zhun-a-zhun-a-zhun.

The husband was still on land, parking the truck, and we were on water, flooding the motor.

"Just stop it," he declared, as we floated toward nothing.

"You'd better start swimming," shouted a passerby who had sympathy for the husband.

I should have been horrified or angry, but I was amused, and the two of us sat in the boat, giggling uncontrollably while the husband was on the brink of a coronary arrest on the bank of the canal.

He calmed himself and gave the daughter more specific directions on cranking.

"Whatever you do, don't laugh," I said to her, and she laughed. Talk about rebellious children. My job was to push the choke on the motor back in place when it cranked.

I, however, never got to do my job.

"We're getting further out in this canal," I observed, when the husband shouted from the shore, "Throw me the rope."

And then as an afterthought, he added, "But hold on to one end of it."

Well, that amused me, too, and I had to sit down and laugh a little bit more with the daughter; we haven't seen each other in a long time, and this is what we do.

"Throw me the rope," he repeated, perhaps secretly wishing we would float out to sea.

"I'll let you do that, cowgirl," I said to the daughter, since I had failed miserably at backing down the ramp.

Her first throw fell short of the mark, just as the husband's blood pressure began to hit a new one.

On the second throw, she re-grouped, envisioned herself as a member of a professional rodeo, and actually lassoed his flip-flop.

"Not bad," said I.

He pulled us toward him, got in the boat with us, and thought all kinds of bad thoughts about the boat's motor as it continued its mumbling, while refusing to crank.

"You want me to pull you,?" said a female friend on a nearby boat. He would have rather had her shoot him, but she only offered towing.

Moments later, the motor fired up. The daughter and I began to breathe again.

We waved goodbye, and entered the wide and welcoming Gulf of Mexico where blue skies prevailed and white clouds floated by. Within the first hour spent at Piney Point, we were glad we went, glad the weather was good, glad the day was a holiday.

Hours later, we collected the son before getting that boat out of the water and he was an exemplary first mate, driving it onto the trailer by the second try.

"I love happy endings," I said to the daughter.

And to me, she replied, "Well that's too bad, because you're standing in a pile of dog doo."

Happy about Herpes?

Who are the happiest people on television?

Those with genital herpes.

The first time I saw the television commercials of happy people with herpes, I just rolled my eyes and allowed the propaganda to vaporize in the room. But now that I've seen these commercials over and over, I feel like I should stand up and represent the Florida Department of Health or Mothers for a Better America, and suggest: having genital herpes is not a good thing.

And that's the nicest way I can think to say it.

On the television commercials, of course, this particular treatment for the disease guarantees you a good-looking date for horseback riding, swimming at waterfalls, additional sex or bicycling at exotic locations.

And then at the very end, in supercalifragilisticexpialidocious form, the announcer reminds that genital herpes can't be cured, continued "outbreaks" may be experienced, and this medication could permanently damage your internal organs.

It's difficult to get in the mood for horseback riding under those circumstances, I would imagine.

So get off that horse, and listen up: television is not always real. If you watch too much, you'll begin to believe that Martin Sheen is President of the United States, and the Terminator is governor of California. Wait, the Terminator *is* the governor of California.

These are strange times in which we live.

Recently, Rush Limbaugh returned to the air waves after previously acknowledging his addiction to prescription drugs and checking himself into a drug rehab center for a month. I was not an avid Rush follower, although I agreed in general terms with the way he catalogued politicians' words side-by-side with their actions.

It was an effective way to set the record straight—only to have it come back and haunt him. Pedestals are now—and always have been—so uncomfortable, and so dangerous.

Martha Stewart is back in the kitchen, although there are many out there who want her working for the rest of her life in the cafeteria line at a prison. I am not among them. I doubt all her financial dealings were strictly legal, but I also believe they would have been largely overlooked and surely more forgiven if she hadn't been female and tremendously successful/powerful. But she's been fair game for as long as she's been raising game and cooking it, too, and the jokes come so easily: she's cooked her goose, you know, and that's not a good thing. Her stock is falling faster than a bad soufflé.

I think business testosterone worldwide was offended when Stewart's dynasty became a public commodity. After all, people who polish silver and collect china shouldn't be found on the New York Stock Exchange, unless they're serving lunch.

Meanwhile, 99 percent of all athletes who make more money than she does, and don't know any more about stock options than I do, fly through society's tangled web unscathed, biting off people's ears and being publicly repentant for being caught in compromising situations with members of the opposite sex. Even with 911 recordings and bloody gloves, we forgive them and bring in the cheerleaders with cleavage.

These are strange times in which we live.

I learned this week that the new trend in naming babies is to visit a car lot and pick out a model you like. There are now 45 children named Infiniti, a number of boys called Chevy, several children who are named after cans in the pantry (that would be Del Monte) and two who were christened, ESPN, pronounced es-pen.

No wonder the happiest people on television appear to be those with genital herpes. These are strange times in which we live.

You Can Call Me "Legs"
... Really, I Don't Mind

I think I'm about to hit a growth spurt.

Not the wide one—I've already hit that one.

I think I'm going to spend the second half of my life as a tall person, and I'm really looking forward to it.

I came to this conclusion after a series of nights experiencing leg pains. Some could say it was too much weight on those feet, or too much time on those feet, or simply aging. But I vividly remember my mother calling them "growing pains," even though I never grew that much. Anyway, I like her diagnosis of "growing pains" and I'm sticking to it.

So, finally, in defiance of medical research, I think I've hit my growth spurt and I'm going to be tall.

I couldn't be happier.

The first thing I'm going to do is audition to be a Rockette and perform at Radio City Music Hall in New York City. I've always wanted to be a Rockette and I'll soon be leaving for The Big Apple to pursue this dream. I'll send you a postcard. Now that I'm tall, I can probably reach the counter in the post office to write a note upon that card.

When I'm not working as a Rockette, I'll come home to clean off the top of my refrigerator. I've hesitated to invite tall people over to my house for 30 years, for I have no clue what they might see ... that I've never seen. I don't know what's on top of the shower stall, or how thick the dust is on the higher window ledges.

I also plan to look 20 pounds thinner and svelte.

Short people never look svelte.

But I am going to be tall and svelte.

I've always felt that another six inches in verticality would improve my appearance significantly. Give me 10 inches in height, and people will say "yes ma'am" to me. God is good ... to grant me more places to put the weight that accumulates with years.

As a tall person, I'm going to hang the pictures in my home higher.

I'm going to clean the chandelier I can't currently reach, and the ceiling fans too.

I'm going to wear dangling earrings and big jewelry, without looking completely ridiculous.

I'm going to live for the day when someone calls me, "Legs," so that I can be "offended" by it.

Being short is not an awful experience; no one accuses you of being "gangly" or having ape-like appendages. But they don't pick you for basketball, either, or offer you the front seat where there's plenty of leg room. On good days, you get a "cute" designation and the back seat in the car over the hump.

But that's about to end. In the tall half of my life, I'm going to wear flared slacks, without alterations taking out the flare.

I'm going to worry that my slacks may be too short after they're washed, like tall people do.

I'm going to buy long torso bathingsuits and wear sandals with heels like those tall "Miss America" contestants do.

I'm going to buy a blazer that doesn't hit me at the knees, and I'm going to wear stripes that go around instead of up and down.

And when Radio City Music Hall calls, I'm going to load up my mother and her two short sisters, and we're going to New York City to marvel together that one member of our family finally had enough legs to make the cut.

Even if she was nearly 50 and just dreaming when it happened. They're right: it is growing pains.

Listen my children and you shall hear: The Greatest Beach Music of All Times

The husband turned the ignition key on the Jeep and the four of us were vacuum-packed for an eight-hour car trip which had been the subject of my nightmares for the previous two weeks.

On this maiden journey to South Carolina, I was the Great Accommodator. I rotated from front to back seat in order to keep law and order; I supplied snacks and replacement batteries; I ignored the ridiculous music which boomed over the radio stations in the three states through which we traveled.

But, by the return trip, the husband and I staged a revolt that went something like this: "We paid for this car; we paid for this trip; we paid for the gas and for the vacation. Find something good to read—gnaw on the car upholstery if you must. The radio now belongs to us."

The children had blank and sad little faces. They looked at each other, wondering how adamantly they should protest, wondering if we'd leave them behind, knowing it was a possibility. The Oldie Goldies were now in command; get your do-wop ready.

Judy Collins sang "Clouds" while the weatherman confirmed the forecast. "The Way You Do The Things You Do" led the husband to break it down in the back seat while the daughter took a turn driving.

"It's too loud," she complained.

"Oh it's fine," we said, taking a page from her book.

"Black Magic Woman" and "Daydream Believer" joined us for the ride as "My Midnight Confession" became the topic of conversation.

They really rolled their eyes when "Hello, Mary Lou, Goodbye Heart" came on and we encouraged them, instead, to tap their toes and enjoy the tunes.

"This Diamond Ring" had a natural pairing with "What Kind of Fool Do You Think I Am?" The question was answered with, "Hit The Road Jack, and Don't You Come Back No More, No More, No More, No More."

We sang our own personal tributes to Ray Charles, whose music forever changed the landscape. "Georgia On My Mind" played as pine trees continued their unending path through the Southeastern United States, intermittently interrupted by blooming magnolias and mimosa trees.

"He Don't Love You, Like I Love You" just begs to be sung aloud, and so we did. We tried to cue the son in for the ah-ooomp in "Natural Woman" by Aretha Franklin, while sharing accolades for Diana Ross and her "Someday, We'll Be Together," closely followed by "I Hear A Symphony … whenever you are near."

Shark and gator tooth jewelry was proffered on billboards along the way as we heard Jose Feliciano lament, "Ain't No Sunshine When She's Gone." She must have been gone on Sunday, for there wasn't "no sunshine."

It was Bible trivia time when "Turn, Turn, Turn" resounded through the airwaves. "What book of the Bible does it come from?" I asked and the children thought it was a trick question. "Listen: To everything there is a season, and a time for every purpose under heaven."

It's Ecclesiastes, or Escalations, depending on your translation.

"Fee-Fi-Fo-Fum, Look Out Baby, Here I Come," was a fitting introduction to "Bad, Bad, Leroy Brown" and I cast my eyes upon the children who asked, "Haven't we already heard that today?"

"No," I assured them.

"All your music sounds alike," they said, which is a criticism they have fielded for their own musical preferences.

"Impossible," I declared. The range was from "Mony, Mony" to "What A Day For A Daydream," to "Dancing in the Moonlight" and "Your

Mama Don't Dance and Your Daddy Don't Rock'n'Roll," while "Nobody was getting fat but Mama Cass."

"Get Ready" was the next song, and we used it as encouragement for the following set of 12 uninterrupted Oldie Goldies.

For the children I sang, "You Didn't Have to Be So Nice; I Would Have Loved You Anyway." I dredged up images of likely candidates for Carly Simon's "You're So Vain" while "Under the Boardwalk" reminded me of the Carolina coastline we had just left behind.

"I'm A Soul Man," became the husband's solo, and we staged a duet of "It Takes Two.... to make a dream come true."

"Ohmigosh," said the son, completely disenchanted by our music, our sentiment and our presentation.

Peaches and Vidalia onions were for sale along the roadside, while Peaches & Herb sang, "Love Is Strange." We performed exotic hand motions for the Temptations' selections, and remarkable facial expressions for Al Green's "So Tired of Being Alone." When "Dead Man's Curve" was played we were on the straight and narrow, watching the oleander bloom right below billboards which announced, "We Bare All." I noted that the apostrophe was incorrectly placed on "toys" and the children just shook their heads. It was a painful time for them, so we encouraged, "Hang On Sloopie" and remember: "I Love You More Today Than Yesterday." So "Give Me One Kiss and I'll be Happy," or "Hold Me Tight."

No takers.

We hardly noticed the State Trooper because, as the station declared, "The Greatest Beach Music of All Times" was being played.

Stevie Wonder crawled in the car with us and a ticket would have been worth it. When Stevie sings, "Signed, Sealed, Delivered, I'm Yours," life is good and movements are required. I'm sure the trooper would have understood.

Cathead River sneaked by us, with Turtle River and Crooked River taking turns at running parallel alongside the Jeep. Elbow Swamp added interest to the landscape while Army convoys reminded us of the serious meaning behind the song, "Soldier Boy."

It was a musical journey of two and, occasionally, four-part harmony, depending on how many people knew the song, or cared. And it was the best remedy for an eight-hour trip, with dedications to the children: "Don't know much about history or the French I took, but I do know that I love you and if you love me too, what a wonderful world it would be."

Yeah, we can get out of the car now. Wasn't that fun?

Adjusted Income is Gross

The husband was holding the income tax packet when he made his droll announcement.

"I think if we get a divorce, we can save enough money in one year to pay off the child's college education and the house."

I just sat there; it was one of those occasions when the proper words didn't come to mind instantly.

"Well, I'm crazy in love with you, too," I said.

I knew, however, that it had nothing to do with love.

It has to do with taxes and what the government considers forgivable and unforgivable. As dysfunctional as we are (and we are), our family is far too normal for the federal government in the United States of America.

We would be better off if I were a single mom, so that I could get federal aid instead of paying it.

Or if I had gone to prison, for there's a foundation that pays for the educational and living expenses of children whose parents have been incarcerated.

Or if I had embezzled money and couldn't remember where I put it, but said I was sorry (and I was kidding).

This staying married to the same person for 23 years and having two children is just off-the-charts now.

"Children by the same two parents," the husband said, as if we'd failed.

"And we work," said the husband, as if we should be ashamed.

"We really should quit that working stuff," I said, and that's long been my argument.

"I could watch Oprah and you could check the mail," I suggested.

"We could move into a smaller house, and both the children's education would be paid for. They could get car loans easy enough, and our parents, well they're just on their own."

We shook our heads in unison, both in dismay and amazement.

I always thought I wanted to be normal, but now that I'm kinda sorta there, it's not so much fun, because you're an entity that defies explanation. Everybody needs a label; we don't have one.

We've brushed by this concept before in our family, but sending the federal government money every April 15 (and each week up to that point) seems to bring the pain and suffering to the surface again.

"Do you remember when the daughter was looking at college scholarships and how we didn't qualify because we weren't Alaskan/Indian, and worse still, we were married, and we were both working ..." and his voice just trailed away, a man broken by discouragement.

It's a terrible thing, Snow White, to awaken and discover that you've done all the right things and you're now being penalized for them. Need a snack? Here's a poison apple.

"Do you realize," he said, "that we can work until middle of April and not one dime we've made is really ours. Tax Freedom Day is in May. Until that day, all the money we make goes to pay state and federal taxes."

I said nothing; I hate to interrupt a bad mood.

"Not one dime," he said. "Why do we bother?"

I started to suggest a vacation up the East Coast so that we could dump some tea into the Boston Harbor, together, but instead I fixed him a stiff Coca-Cola and pushed him toward the door.

"Nobody's helping us," I reminded him.

"Not the government, not society, not nobody," I said, and I had a particularly good time voicing that double negative; it seemed fitting for his mood, also a double negative.

"So get yourself back up to that office," I said.

"And go to work."

(For the government.)

Boy,
Oh
Boy!

If a Dog is 'Man's Best Friend,' Shouldn't Man Be Doing This?

"Wipe your paws," I said to the dog before we entered the veterinarian's office. We were there for her annual check-up and she didn't have a clue.

I maintain that she rides in cars better than the children ever did—she notices the flowers blooming on the roadside, and gets excited about seeing other dogs in town. It's like Christopher Columbus' first glimpse of the New World.

Upon our arrival, we interrupted a true celebration in the veterinarian's office. Two families had gathered to see—for the first time—nine new grandpuppies, the product of an arranged marriage between two chocolate labs. Everyone was ecstatic. Even the great grandparents had gathered.

Right in the midst of this family gathering, they called my dog's name and we entered the examination room. As it turns out, she doesn't even like the scale. It reminds her of the boys in the neighborhood trying to hoist her onto their four-wheelers. She's got more sense than to ride with them, and she doesn't want to ride the scale either.

But with some coaxing, we determined that she was 51.3 pounds. That 51.3 pounds would soon be working against me.

It reminded me of "well baby" visits in the pediatrician's office where nurses with bright smiles tell you how well-adjusted your baby is, and how nicely he or she is growing.

They bragged on the dog's temperament; "she's a good dog," they said, "and there's nothing finer than a good dog." We talked about her adoption which was arranged by their office.

"We are still very grateful," I said, remembering how our pet of 14 years died only days before the Christmas of 2003. The new pet was eight weeks old and looked great with a red bow around her neck.

Now she's a full-grown woman dog; she's been fixed; and she's quite happy with her life in the country. So why in the world did I take her to a place where they use needles with such regularity?

After a couple of vaccinations and a stool sample, the dog was a different dog. Then the doctor cleaned her ears, two or three times each. There was a look of desperation in her brown eyes.

Having had some sinus trouble of my own, I had to ask, "Can you put some of that in my ears?" I know professionals of his genre can typically treat humans too.

"I could," he said, "but you might start chasing cars, and too many people would recognize you."

When his assistant finally announced, "She's great; you can go now," the dog leapt off the scale and used all 51.3 pounds to drag me down the hallway in the wrong direction. I was skiing on the linoleum and trying to remain calm.

"Whoooaaa," I said, tugging at her leash. "Let's go this way." It was quite a field trip to the front office. In the reception area, where the check would be written, there was a boxer who appeared capable of consuming me and my dog. There was also a little pooch in his owner's arms. I immediately determined that he would not be a threat.

My dog, who obviously hasn't learned all the survival skills that a dog needs in this world, thinks all dogs surely love her, because everybody she knows loves her. She wanted to play. I instantly perceived that the other dog did not want to play. His owner was desperately trying to restrain him, while I attempted to calm my pet, too.

I tightened up on her leash and went to retrieve my checkbook, when my dog just wrapped me up with her leash——round, and round, and round, from my ankles to my knees.

"Oh great," I said, sure that I would soon be on the floor of the veterinarian's office with at least two dogs on top of me.

I made a few mental notes: write the check before the vaccinations, never wear something you need to wear beyond the veterinarian's visit, or better yet, ask the husband to make the next trip (and don't tell him why).

On our way out the door, my dog lunged toward the dog I had been avoiding, and I lunged in the opposite direction, dropping the heartworm medicine, but getting my beast out of the office. The other dog owner—a sweet, young friend from long ago—retrieved the heartworm medicine while multi-tasking with her own pet, and I breathed for the first time in eight minutes.

"What are you doing?" I asked the dog who seemed to want to race down the adjacent highway. She was pulling me through the parking lot in the opposite direction of those scales and needles.

"Get in this car," I commanded and she did.

I fussed at her all the way to the baseball field, then I lowered the window to see whose uniforms I could identify, and it seemed that the animal was going to jump out. So I raised the window back ... sandwiching her head between the window and the car frame.

She yelped mightily and I was horrified. How would I explain this to the family?

I quickly released the window and the dog jumped from the front seat to the far back with the golf clubs and foldable chairs.

She stayed as far away from me as she could for the remainder of the ride home, and I couldn't have been happier. We didn't speak for two hours and I had to wonder if Columbus' first glimpse of the New World didn't end up like this. First you see the flora and the fauna, and you smile, and the next thing you know the hostile natives jump out of the bushes, scalp your friends and steal your oars.

Welcome to the New World. Now you need shots.

Covering the Bases

We spent the Fourth of July of the year 2002 close to Home Plate, beginning the day with cereal and batting practice.

By Friday, the Fifth of July, we were well on our way to First Base in Live Oak, Fla.., at the Suwannee County Sports Complex. It was our first game in the State Babe Ruth Championship Tournament for 9-year-olds. The game wasn't a cake walk, but the outcome was what we had longed for. We traveled home with a smile upon our faces.

By Saturday, the Sixth of July, we were at Second Base and on the right side of a 15-0 score.

By Sunday, the Seventh of July, we were at Third Base and there was trouble at the O.K. Corral. We lost once; we lost twice; and the umpire said, "You're outta here."

We wouldn't be sliding into Home Plate to the sounds of victory.

We would be sliding home.

My team is not unlike your team. I can easily walk through the line-up, and speak of the players' varying athletic abilities and their interesting personalities. Or I can tell you about temper, about compassion, about their loyalty and their perseverance.

You don't want to know everything these boys are thinking; you don't want to know everything these boys are saying. They can't always be trusted to keep up with their hats, their batting averages, or their gastrointestinal malfunctions.

But it occurred to me Sunday, when Third Base became our last, that these young athletes care about the game for so many of the right reasons. They believe in trying hard, sweating, working tirelessly and showing off skillfully when given the opportunity.

For less than $2.8 million annually.

Considerably less.

Actually, for fun.

For the sake of competition.

For the opportunity to hang out with their friends and develop a skill.

In the heat of the moment Sunday, the agony of defeat was deeply felt throughout the team and its extended family of relatives, friends and die-hard fans. We had come so far and practiced so much, it seemed possible—if not fair—that we'd find ourselves in the regional competition. But that started slipping away from us Sunday morning, and continued on a downhill trend.

I looked around at the adults I had spent the summer with; they are as interesting as their players and as much fun, too. While each of us may breathe a sigh of relief for a more relaxed schedule, I doubt any of us will continue our days and nights without missing—a little bit—the others with whom we had shared the summer sun. I know I won't.

Sunday afternoon, late, when I was about to let melancholy take over the day, I listened carefully and heard the baseball being bounced off the side of the house, and then off the roof. Over and over again. I looked out: boy, glove, ball, dog. Tournament or not, the pace continues.

None of these boys who have won my heart and admiration will likely earn $2.8 million playing the sport professionally.

But all will have learned how to love the sport, and have it love you back.

And that is perhaps the real grand slam of baseball.

Glass Houses and
Paneful Sentiment

It's been about a year since the older child wistfully pronounced: "He's a lot of fun if you can watch him through a window."

She was, of course, referring to her younger brother—a source of pride and aggravation intermittently.

I found it to be a curious statement, but I had no idea of its profound reach until a cold January Sunday.

On that day, I watched the four-year-old through glass. Without anyone to observe, monitor or correct, he played happily ... scurrying from the wheelbarrow to the fishing boat, from the bicycle to the swings, over and through other objects with which he played enthusiastically.

And I found myself saying, "He's a lot of fun if you can watch him through a window."

Windows are good friends, of course. They restrict your awareness of whining and thus improve your attitude. They limit your interference into the "work" of play, and allow you to watch, unhindered, the backyard version of the Indy 500, landscaping detail work, or a war of the worlds in the sandbox.

Windows can frame your family-in-motion like a movie camera would, always improving the view.

"Oh he's growing up," I said rather sadly to no one in particular, as I leaned on the windowsill. The young one flew out of the driveway on a bicycle, challenging the speed of light. The dog raced to get out of his way, and almost ran into the sister who was go-carting in a different direction.

The husband came in and found me affixed to the window, searching for a tissue.

"What's wrong?" he asked.

A sigh. "The children are really growing up," I said, still peering out the window.

He was quiet and then must have felt obligated to speak.

"I thought you wanted them to grow up," he said, and I found it to be an unnecessary comment.

Of course I want them to grow up, but not right at this minute when I feel like crying.

Later that same day, there was no window to be found and I knew I would retract—if not regret—my earlier sentiment.

The children were underfoot, tangled up in my apron strings, complaining about food and friends and foes.

As I loaded the dishwasher and landed on a bow-and-arrow which caused me to trip over the older daughter's lunchbox still packed with two-day-old carnage, I gestured toward the heavens for help, protection and, yes, deliverance.

"Yeah, the children are really growing up," the husband said in jolly skepticism.

And I found it to be an unnecessary comment. So I shot him with the bow-and-arrow, and wondered to myself: "Would he be more fun on the other side of a window?"

Who are the True
Fishing Optimists?

It is with foreign curiosity that I watch the boys prepare for any fishing trip. They don't even know I'm looking.

We played baseball until 10:15 one Friday night, and then returned home to a frantic "get ready for the Optimist Club tournament" work night which involved miles of fishing line and steady planning.

"Where are we going in the boat first?" asked the son, who was making piles of used line on the floor and putting "fresh line" on the reels. I can't tell you the father's answer, except to say that it involved "local waters."

"And then where?" the son inquired, as the father completed an inventory of the hooks and lures within the tackle box—too close to the daughter's white sorority formal which is still languishing on the pool table while we attempt to find a place for all her worldly belongings before she returns to college again in two months.

I grabbed the white dress and only got intent stares from both members of the family with a "y" chromosome.

"Can you get us together some drinks?" the father asked, and I knew I should have stayed on that couch. So I grabbed up a half dozen waters and Gatorades, as well as some snacks and remembered not to include napkins. The boys are offended when I add napkins; plus, it's a waste of paper.

At 11:45 p.m., the boys trudged up the stairs to bed, setting their alarms for the big tournament.

"I wouldn't mind going out on the boat and getting some sun," I interjected, since no one had asked.

"Fine," the husband said. "We're leaving at 5 a.m."

Forget that; even the sun's not interested.

The next thing I remember, was the alarm and that herd of cattle going down my stairs.

Then I returned to sleep and couldn't help but be happy that I wasn't getting any sun. For I was getting some peace and quiet, and we can all thank the Optimists for that, once a year.

I was just settling into my favorite couch for morning t.v., when the son appeared at the patio window.

My heart dropped. "The husband's dead," I thought.

I rushed to the window and the boy's face was a sad one.

"The boat wouldn't work," he said, with obvious disappointment. "Never could get it to crank," he added, shaking his head. I looked to the side yard and the husband was venting …

"I am so…." I'll let you finish the sentence, but it was an animated expression of both anger and disgust. His protest continued: "We've been up since 5 a.m…." and I'll let you finish that sentence too.

Like a good Jewish mother, I said, "Can I get you something to eat?"

It was the only thing I could think to say.

"We don't want to eat," said the husband. "We want to fish."

"Well, since I can't fix the motor, is there anything else I can do?"

"We just came back to get the little boat, and we're going again," said the boy.

"In the john boat?" I asked.

"Yeah," he said.

They pulled out the smaller motor for that boat and it cranked the first time.

"You can fix us some peanut butter and jelly sandwiches," said the husband, instructing the son to remove the contents of the big boat and to pare them down for the little boat.

The father hoisted the little boat into the back of the truck, with sheer adrenaline and rage, and within 30 minutes, they were gone again.

"Poor boys," I said aloud, as I settled into my couch again, watching their dust settle in the driveway.

Ten minutes later, the daughter—who had an overnight babysitting job—arrived in their dust.

"Can I have the couch?" she asked. "I am so tired."

I gave up my couch and decided that the Optimist Tournament had not proven to be as much fun as I had hoped. I fed my disappointment by going to the grocery store and running three errands.

When I returned home early afternoon, the truck and the little boat were parked in the side yard.

I knew this couldn't be good.

"We got out about 300 yards, and the little motor wouldn't crank," said the husband between snores and sighs. "I had to paddle us in against the current, load the stupid boat back on the truck ..."

"Oh no," I said, again, feeling his pain. "It cranked this morning," I remembered.

"I know," he said, resisting the urge to bite my head off at that moment.

"The boy was going to get out and push, and it looked like a Tarzan movie with alligators sliding off the banks into the water." He just shook his head; I thought he might cry. "We've been up since 5 a.m., out twice with two different boats. It's 2 p.m. and we haven't even wet a hook."

"I'll fix you a big dinner," said I, and how did I grow up Jewish in the Baptist church?

"No, we're going again," he said.

"You're out of boats," I reminded him.

"And we're out of the tournament," he was sure, "but I've never let a fish stump me before and I won't today either."

Two hours later, they loaded up for local waters within a local hunting club. And they caught fish—good fish. They came home after dark—smiling and overlooking the previous horror of the day.

If the Optimist Tournament had a category for optimistic fishermen, they would have won. It took two boats, two motors, six bags of ice and 14 hours, but as eternal optimists, they conquered the finned species.

And beat their chests.

It was a small step for a man and his boy, but a giant leap for all testosterone.

We
Gather
Together

Checkmate

There is much to be learned around the table at Thanksgiving Dinner.

Whether a conscious effort or not, upon marrying an individual, you spend considerable time wondering about his/her family's sanity rating. I say this openly for I'm sure my efforts in this matter have been matched by my husband's.

In fact, it's a chess game of sorts, and I don't think I'm the only one who plays.

For this particular Thanksgiving, the games began at my mother's house, gravitating from her table to others' within my family.

One of the grandchildren had a term paper due on Monday. "Why, we can help you with it," said the 70-year-old trio of sisters, in melodic and generous Southern voices.

"No, no, no," said the student's father. "I made a 'D' on the term paper they helped me with."

I smiled adoringly at The Sisters and asked my cousin, "You knew they went to a double-header this week, didn't you?"

"Baseball?" he asked.

"No, a funeral in the morning in Montgomery, Ala., and one in the afternoon in Selma."

He shook his head, chuckled, and poked at the fire in the fireplace until he realized it was gas logs.

"Well, I wondered why the room wasn't filled with smoke," he said. "I've never known you to have a fire in this room without it looking like the furniture was smoldering."

Another family member chimed in, "Remember the Thanksgiving we painted Mama's house?"

And a detractor spoke up. "Y'all didn't even take the screens out when you painted; it was the biggest mess I've ever seen …"

In my family, you laugh to survive. And if you don't laugh, well then, you may not survive.

"I never will forget when I was about to take off in our small-engine airplane and Daddy handed me the parts he had never put back on the plane after working on it the day before …" said a son recalling the early stages of his father's Alzheimer's.

There's nothing funny about Alzheimer's, and there's nothing funny about missing airplane parts, but there is something comforting about recalling a shared past.

And you'd might as well laugh.

The husband is never so bold as to criticize my family openly, but his subliminal messages are evident to me, for we've been married for thousands of years, and I know these things.

So, as he makes "Not normal, not normal," assessments of statements and stories, I'm getting killed in this imaginary chess game which seeks for normality.

Then the tables turn, literally. I'm at his mother's table hearing about the time one son brought a live turkey home in the back seat of his car. All the way from Tennessee.

"Best turkey we ever had," she said.

Not normal.

Her story for this Thanksgiving, however, involved someone associated with the family only through marriage, not direct blood lines. (There is loyalty around the dinner table, but in-laws are always fair game.)

"Well, let me tell you …" the mother-in-law said succinctly, "that Darlene called to say that Michael took his mother home to Tennessee after she died."

I nodded affirmatively in a dutiful daughter-in-law manner and suggested that this was a thoughtful thing to do.

She looked me straight in the eyes and said, "No. I mean he wrapped her up, put her in the back of the truck and drove her from Florida to Tennessee after the woman was dead."

"He did what?" I blurted out, and the brothers stopped passing the cornbread dressing in mid-air. All eyes were upon her.

She went into detail about the route they took, passing stores the mother had patronized and favorite scenic overlooks.

"She was dead in the back of the truck?" I asked. "Isn't that illegal?"

"Could you pass the cranberry sauce, please?"

"What would he have said if he was stopped for some traffic violation?"

More sweet potatoes, please.

"Have you ever?" asked the mother-in-law, knowing that she had won Story of the Day.

"Never," I admitted.

And at that moment, I caught the attentive eye of the husband who had looked curiously at my family for 24 hours.

He shook his head; we shared one of those moments for which you need a flavored coffee.

And I had to declare mentally, "Checkmate."

I think he heard me.

Driving Miss Daisy

A special wedding lured our family to Alabama for this particular weekend in February, prompting us to travel hundreds of miles, packed between suits and dresses for every occasion.

We had a two-hour "layover" at the Grandmother's house before we traveled to the first festivity, which was in a performing arts center another 50 miles away.

The daughter said "hello" to us on her way to the shower, having traveled solo from a college campus to the Grandmother's house where I draped clothes from room to room, as I shifted boys to one area and girls to another.

We were to leave for the first event at 6 p.m., but we all knew what that meant; we had discussed it in advance. The Grandmother knows nothing about being "fashionably late." She adheres to the philosophy that "Earliness is next to godliness," and if she says we're leaving at 6 p.m., she'll have her heels and hose on by 5 p.m. and be sitting on the couch with her purse on her arm at 5:30…. looking at her watch.

The best way to be remembered fondly is to be sitting there with her by 5:45 p.m.

"And another thing," I said to the husband, who fancies himself a modern-day Lewis and/or Clark. "You just need to pretend you're the chauffeur; I'm sure you know a better way to go, but you must drive the course she charts." And I quickly added, "Please, oh please."

He agreed in advance, but sat on the couch on the day of the party saying, "Well, wouldn't it be better if…."

And I gave him a silent admonition with raised eyebrows as I shook my head.

"Well," she said graciously. "We went this way Sunday when we went to look at the gifts—they had the bridal dress, which has been worn by four brides before her, on a mannequin in the foyer to the house, and it is beautiful. The gifts? The gifts were lovely—they were everywhere. Anyway," she said, gathering her thoughts, "I wrote down the directions and I think this is probably the best way to go—even though it is a two-lane road. You can't set your cruise control, and there are deer everywhere, but if we are careful, it's the quickest route."

"What if we ..." the husband began, as I flailed my arms in the background, behind the grandmother.

"Never mind," he said. "I'm sure we can get there."

When we piled in the car, we put the boys in front and the girls in the back. It was dark. The Grandmother sat with dignity in her fur. Out of her evening bag, she brought forth a flashlight with hand-penned directions rubber-banded around the handle. I immediately titled our trip, "A Fur, A Flashlight, and a Family of Five."

"Go straight by Cambrian Ridge," she said to Lewis and/or Clark. Given our circumstances, I thought it beneficial to be traveling with someone who understands the significance of moss growing on one side of the tree, and can tell the time by the sun. I just see spots.

The son was riding "shotgun" to look out for deer. Between the trip there and our return four hours later, we saw 13 deer ... and hit none.

The husband had polished up on his "yes ma'am's" and was doing just fine until he came upon a barricade with orange and white stripes which said, "Bridge out; road closed to thru traffic."

"Oh, you can just go through that," the Grandmother said.

"Well, I don't know...." he said, stumbling around in thought, wondering if it was better to break the law or defy the mother-in-law.

"It was fine on Sunday," she said. "They've got clay piled up over the creek bed and it's just fine."

"But it's rained all week," he said, moving forward an inch and then braking again, knowing that if we got stuck, he was the only one in the car to get us out.

"Just go right on through," she said, pointing with her flashlight, and that was the final word.

The husband dutifully obeyed, but not without first catching my attention and silently suggesting that this was surely worth a fishing trip or 18 holes of golf.

We proceeded without incident until a second set of barricades appeared. "Bridge out, 1.5 miles," the sign said and the husband balked again.

"I just don't know," he said. "Where I'm from, if the sign says 'Bridge out,' you take the detour."

"If you take that detour, you'll go 20 miles out of your way," the Grandmother explained, turning on the flashlight to look at her watch.

"And we're only an hour early now," said the daughter who embraces the concept of "fashionably late" and can never get to the couch quickly enough to sit with the Grandmother.

The husband had been hung out to dry and we all knew it, but he knew it best. He continued down the road as the Grandmother directed with her flashlight. The third and final barricade appeared. It couldn't have been more dramatic if God had sent an angel in an orange vest, straight from heaven to sit upon our hood.

"Bridge out. Detour," the sign said with an arrow pointing to the right.

"Just ease on in there, and if it's bad, we'll turn around," said the Grandmother from the back seat. He loosened his tie and eased forward. Silence fell upon the car, as we braced ourselves for imminent doom.

Sure enough, there was adequate clay piled up over the river bed, that we just traveled right over that creek, looking at the drop-off from either side.

"You can't even tell it's rained," the son declared, both surprised and disappointed.

"See," the Grandmother said, not missing a beat. She turned on her flashlight and continued, "Now take County Road 41. There's a brick house where you turn left."

When we arrived at our appointed destination, I patted the husband on the back, handed him something cool to drink and introduced him.

"Is this your husband?" a distant relative asked.

"Actually, he's our chauffeur," I said. That's when I was on the receiving end of a silent admonition with raised eyebrows. And now I'm thinking that his fishing trip may have to be all the way to Australia, with 18 holes of golf at St. Andrews in Scotland, on the way.

At least.

How Many Miss Daisy's
Must One Man Drive?

As luck would have it, the husband ended up as the chauffeur for not one, not two, not three, but four women on a busy Saturday night in downtown Austin, Texas, where newspaper friends had gathered for an annual convention.

The confusion presented by six lanes of traffic was compounded by a healthy pedestrian population, police officers on bicycles, and street vendors hawking tortillas and frozen drinks.

It was nothing, however, compared to the confusion within the car.

Seeing friends once a year—maybe twice—makes for convoluted conversation, at best, as you try to piece together what was new last year with what is current this year.

"So is Amanda dating the same boy?" I asked, knowing that this particular young man was a major blip on the radar at last year's get-together.

"Oh yes," said the mother with arched eyebrows and careful composure.

"He's the punter, right?" the husband asked, trying to remember the blip. And then he added for the rest of us, "He had the best punting record in the nation for all college punters last year."

The reaction was an animated chorus of "wowwwww," and "oh reallllly?" and even an, "Is that soooo?"

"He's in New York now, trying out for the Buffalo Bills," the mother said.

"He's a free agent," the husband interjected.

"Ohhhh, wowwwww, I seeeeee," the female chorus sang again.

"I wonder how far he's had to kick it through the goal posts," said one woman in the back seat, clutching her purse as women will do.

The husband paused, wondering whether to be polite or to strive for accuracy, and then he jumped in.

"No," he said, trying to re-arrange our thinking. "He punts—he doesn't do field goals or extra points. His specialty is punting."

"So his objective," I explained, "is to kick it as close to the zero line as he can, without getting it over the line."

The husband nearly came to a complete stop on the Texas Freeway. As the lights from highway signs pulsed off and on like a strobe, separating the darkness from the light, he cocked his head and repeated, "The zero line? Where in the world have you heard it called the zero line?"

I knew I had let him down and, granted, the "zero line" didn't sound right to me, either. "But that's what it is, isn't it?" I asked him. "If you count in a descending order from 10, it is the zero line—the one over which you score."

The back seat was consumed with laughter ... friendly laughter. We had laughed this way through meetings and malls, through beef tenderloin and Tex-Mex enchiladas.

He put on his blinker while shaking his head.

"Most folks call it the goal line," he said.

And they all chimed in. "That's right—the goal line." More laughter. More oohing and ahhing. I knew the husband was in Female Purgatory and would rather be chained to the tampon aisle at a department store.

"Well, I'll bet he has one nice leg," said the friend clutching her purse.

I tried not to laugh, but I couldn't help myself. It was like a middle age spend-the-night party.

"I'll bet he has two," said I, wondering how effective a kicker would be with just one.

Well, it didn't take much with this group. They were doubled over with laughter, and patting the husband in a friendly way, hoping he was enjoying the ride as much as they were.

"I don't know why I said that," said the woman with the purse. Even in the dark, I could see her blush.

"Are you still thinking about her daughter's boyfriend's legs?" I had to ask, and the back seat was out of control.

After moments dedicated to regaining composure, another rider asked, "Well, what happens if he does kick it over the zero?"

The husband was descending deeper into hell, as the speedometer on the rental car kept time.

"It's not the zero," he said. "It's the goal line," and that was no reason to laugh hysterically, but these women didn't need a reason. They laughed hysterically and loved him for driving them around, for putting up with their nonsense in a jovial manner.

"If he does kick it over the goal, it comes back out to the 20-yard-line," the husband said, trying to keep a straight face and surely wondering how much further, before he could punt.

The chorus began again. "That's right," they said in unison, having recalled that detail from 50 previous football seasons where they stared at the t.v. and wondered how the majorettes stayed so slim.

"Oh, this is so much fun," said one to the others, shifting her purse and pulling down her skirt.

And just when she was enjoying herself the most, the artistically lighted lodge appeared on the horizon at Lake Travis, rising like a Phoenix to welcome the husband from the ashes of his crumbled world. Here, where deer horns formed the chandeliers, there would be men who knew about pitching and politics, about printing presses and prime rib.

And punting.

He was at the zero line, having driven four Miss Daisy's well.

Lost and Found

My cousin Stephen is finding himself.

That's what the aunts said at Christmas when he was noticeably absent from our circle of family. He's changed colleges; he's changed jobs; he's changed girlfriends.

With spellbound intensity, the circle of cousins uttered a collective and knowing, "Really?"

With all these changes, my aunts are confident that something positive is on the horizon for Stephen. "He's finding himself," they said with certainty.

It caused me to ponder: I never remember losing myself. It seems I've always known pretty much where I was, even if I didn't like it.

My father was reasonably clear about the purpose of college, and thus I started my first job three days after I graduated. If push-had-come-to-shove, he might have extended a grace period for me, but I wasn't inclined to find that out. He never had the privilege of attending college, and he delineated his belief that if he had saved all those thousands of dollars for me to obtain higher learning, then I'd better be willing to exhibit the fruits of that learning.

"Yes sir," was always a good thing to say to my father.

And that's what I said.

It's nice to know how far you can push someone, and that may have been a more important lesson than English 101, but everything is higher learning, if you treat it that way.

So I've looked back on those years I spent away at college, and the family gatherings I missed. I am now reasonably certain that the aunts sat around and talked about me finding myself.

To them, it probably appeared that I was lost. For I went to college to be a biologist. I then decided I liked the idea of interior design. I thought I might want to be a stewardess on a French-American flight so I got a minor in French. I also got one in religion. Then I switched to journalism and at Christmas, the aunts asked, "You're going to chase ambulances for stories?"

Another said, "We've never had a writer in our family," as if to suggest that if there's never been one, there probably isn't the basis for such.

I now know that they politely waited until I left to suggest, "Susan's trying to find herself."

Pass the tissues.

So when I hear this same sentiment about Stephen, I have a different perspective. I don't feel the slightest pang of sympathy or empathy for him. I don't need a tissue. But I do admit to a hint of jealousy.

For, back in the 70s when the aunts were lamenting how lost I was, I was thinking how "found" I felt. The world was mine, and I was sure of it. So they can worry about Stephen if they wish.

Instead, I'm going to transport myself back to the 1700s when Daniel Boone roamed this countryside. While his aunts sat around at Christmas and suggested that he was obviously trying to find himself, he maintained, "I have never been lost, but I will admit to being confused for several weeks."

There is absolutely nothing wrong with a long walk in the forest.

The Princess and the Pea

When the daughter was leaving home after Thanksgiving, we stood in agreement at the foot of her bed.

"You need a new mattress," I said, and she nodded.

There's nothing wrong with her current mattress except that it's 27 years old. It's the first one I bought when I left home, got a job and began a career that I thought would last a few years ... before I got rich, famous or was taken care of in the manner to which I had grown accustomed.

Twenty-seven years later, the daughter is still using that mattress, but needs a new one, and I'm still going to work most days.

"Give me until Christmas break, and I'll get you one," said I.

Christmas, as you know, has a way of hitting you like a baseball bat between the eyes. The night before she arrived home again, I remembered my promise, and realized I had neither the time nor the money to fulfill it.

She complained not one word about the mattress which throws you from either side of the bed to the middle where you sink helplessly. I was grateful for that; after all, there were presents under the tree and I didn't think she'd get real excited about a mattress with a red ribbon upon it.

I didn't feel too badly until we arrived at the first grandmother's house on our holiday excursion.

"You girls have the sleeper sofa," said the grandmother to my daughter and her first cousin.

Their faces were downtrodden.

"I'm not sleeping there again," said the cousin, a little presumptuous to be sure, but polite enough.

"We slept there at Thanksgiving and it was horrible. What about the twin mattresses you've stored under the guest room bed?" the cousin asked.

The grandmother smiled sweetly. "Honey, we've got 12 people sleeping here tonight. I need you girls to sleep on the pull-out sofa."

This particular sleeper sofa has a large hump at what would be the equator if the mattress were a hemisphere. You can hardly choose sides, you just have to fold yourself in half at the waistline like a Barbie doll.

If you pad the bed (which we tried) to elevate the head, then you sleep as if you were on the side of a mountain.... very carefully. Your feet go numb within a couple of hours and you have bad dreams. Some of them come true.

If you prop up the foot of the bed—trying to rid the mattress of its equatorial hump—all the blood rushes to your head and you feel faint.

So we put the girls in the bed sideways. Even as short as they are, their feet dangled a bit at the ends. The hump at the equator nicely defined the sides and, once sleep came, neither could tell the other was on the same mattress. Nor did they brag about a good night's rest.

The next day, the girls begged their aunt (who lives 45 miles from this grandmother's house) to please go home. We love you; we love our gifts; can we have your bed? She was quick to relent and they reported a good night's sleep with pillows which make you stand up and salute.

"Life is rarely perfect," I tried to explain. "At least you got a good mattress ... and if you're really quick you can have the bathroom now too."

Distraction is one of my finer parenting skills.

The next day, we packed our suitcases again for the second grandmother's house.

She met us at the back door to hug our necks and direct the husband who dragged in all our worldly belongings in oversized suitcases.

"Listen, sweetie," she said to the daughter. "I still haven't gotten a new mattress, so I need you to sleep in that back bedroom."

I shouldn't have laughed, but the daughter's countenance drooped so dramatically ... and so did her good nature, not to mention her shoulders. It seemed to be a Mattress Conspiracy and she was at the center of it.

"What about him?" said the daughter pointing at her brother.

"Well, he has the twin bed and I haven't changed the sheets on it since your last visit. The back bedroom has fresh sheets ..."

"And the worst mattress in the world except for the one I just slept on and, of course, that other one at my own house. I'm going to be permanently disfigured," she moaned.

"You'll be fine," I assured her. "It's just two nights and we'll give you the bathroom first with endless hot water and the first pick of the towels. You can use all of them if you want to."

Remembering from our last visit that this mattress would throw an unsuspecting sleeper off the left side like a bucking bronco, she built a replica of the Great Wall of China out of pillows and and their shams to prevent her from rolling off the side to imminent doom.

A night light was missing from the stand, so I handed her a flashlight and a copy of a story I thought she might enjoy: The Princess and the Pea. It's Hans Christian Andersen's story of a princess, countless mattresses and a mundane dried pea.

I looked desperately for a moral, suggesting that this princess who slept fitfully ended up marrying the prince and lived happily ever after.

The daughter eyed me skeptically. "Oh yeah," she said, with her face smashed into the mattress, noting that no one had read her a bedtime story in at least 13 years.

The real moral to the story emerged when we completed our full circle and found ourselves—1000 miles later—back in our home in Perry, Fla. The daughter awakened the next morning, stretched, smiled and declared: "That mattress is not so bad after all."

And, without a doubt, we're going to live happily ever after.

The Mother Lode

In my effort to align the planets between three generations, Mother's Day weekend found me traveling at 70 m.p.h. to my home state to wish the matriarch of my family a happy day. The third generation traveled from her college to sing the second verse of this same song.

In advance, my cousin and I made plans to take "the mothers" we love to lunch in a restaurant accompanying a swank new golf course in the community—part of the Robert Trent Jones trail—which affords spectacular views on a ridge called Cambrian. It also affords good food and we thought it to be the perfect place.

Fourteen things tried to interfere, including the death of a cousin and a 2 p.m. funeral that day. We trudged forward, however, believing that life is at least as important as death, and we put on our Sunday-best to say "Happy Mother's Day."

My aunt was particularly cheerful when we met her and the cousin at the best table in the restaurant. I figured she must have on a $2 dress—nothing makes her happier than to find a $2 designer dress.

So I braced myself for the story to follow, for there is always a story to follow. But instead of a shopping-find, the news involved food. The cousin and her mother whispered, and looked like the proverbial cats after a fine meal of canary.

"Mothers eat free," said the aunt, raising her eyebrows and reigning victorious.

The cousin who had arranged this outing with me, looked curiously at me.

"That's nice," I said, thinking Mother's Day should prompt some special observance.

Then my aunt started pointing fingers, going around the circular table and counting. "We're all mothers," she said, trying to make this coup plain for me. "Except for one," she added, pointing to my daughter.

"Oh," I said, feeling downright awful for the restaurant. "We can't do that."

"Did you know?" I asked my aunt point-blank. It was Mother's Day, I realized, but it was not beyond the realm of possibility that she might have arranged this frugal celebration.

"Why no, I didn't know," she said, acting horrified, "but it says it right up there on the board. And they have Poppy Seed Chicken Casserole, too."

Well, glory be.

The waitress came around and explained the special day. "Mothers eat free," she said, enjoying her role as the bearer of good news.

There was silence.

"We're feeling extremely guilty," I admitted, "because we're all mothers, except for my daughter. So we can't possibly eat free. We'll just let this count for the two grandmothers here."

She paused for a moment and then gave us her decision. "No," she said, with poise and composure. "It's for all mothers, and if you're mothers, you eat free."

I was speechless and looked toward my cousin to object. She was silent which pleased her own mother on Mother's Day.

"I told you," said my aunt, just gloating.

"Well, we have had two parties here," I continued in my discourse with the waitress, hoping to convince her of our assured patronage.

"And we will be back again," said the cousin to my right.

"You help yourselves and have a Happy Mother's Day," she said and she was graceful under pressure, but as a small business owner, it wasn't a stretch for me to realize that it wasn't her food she was giving away.

The grandmothers, who lived through the Depression and still fear another one before they depart this life, delicately removed their plates from the table and proceeded to the buffet line. The food looked all the better, knowing the price.

"Can I plan a luncheon, or can I plan a luncheon?" asked my cousin quietly as she pushed me toward the buffet line, holding my elbow.

I pivoted toward her, almost suspecting that the trickle-down effect of genes had affected her better judgment. "You called, and you knew," I accused, as if I was the prosecutor on the case.

"I did not," she said, offended. "I fully expected to pay. But it's the rule that mothers eat free, and we shall eat free."

I eyed her suspiciously through the rest of the meal, as we enjoyed the chicken along with pork tenderloin, a green salad, a green bean casserole, mashed potatoes, fresh yeast rolls and apple pie for dessert.

We heaped praise upon the manager, the waitresses and each other. The cousin and I slipped generous tips on the table when the grandmothers weren't looking, for they would have removed them.

"It was wonderful," said my aunt, walking toward the front door.

And it was. Anytime you get several generations of women relatives together, the stories pass around the table like potatoes, and the memories get sweet like the tea.

We may never again make our mothers as happy as we did on this Mother's Day when five of us ate for $8.97.

So Mary, Quite Contrary:
how does your cell phone ring?

If I want a reminder of how plain I am, all I have to do is spend time with my friends.

My friends, you see, are among the most colorful, most interesting people on the planet. I sit in awe as I watch them transform themselves and transform the circumstances in which they live.

I don't think I do that so well.

I don't change the color of my lipstick; I don't read books that are out of my comfort zone; and if I get a chance to leave my day-to-day routine, I find myself returning to the same weekend getaway destinations year after year, like a homing pigeon.

I'm just a homing pigeon wearing Toasted Almond lipstick.

I was pondering that thought last week as I looked around at the faces of friends who had gathered around me. One was heading to Vermont to watch the leaves turn colors. Another had on gold shoes. Still another had lost weight and found new jeans.

"What is wrong with me?" I had to ask.

I didn't ask it out loud, though, for although this is a sweet group of people, they might have told me.

First they would have said, "Nothing's wrong with you; you're perfect" because they're nice that way.

But then, someone with an honorable agenda, would have said, "But you might consider Pink Tigress lipstick, or painting those fingernails. Your purse looks like spring and summer; you need a new one. Have you had your nails done lately? Quit cleaning your house and hire someone else to do it."

These women are not without opinions; in fact, they probably have more opinions than they do shoes. And that's a lot.

But instead of asking the question aloud, I pondered it silently as I heard about growing children and growing debts.

This group never gets too quiet, but the conversation lulled as our fearless leader led us through calendars and committees, asking "Does anybody need meals or help?" I'm always proud of the Casserole Brigade which springs into action for sickness and grief.

We were deep into compassion and kindness when—out of the blue—we hear the resounding chords of the Marvin Gaye hit from the 70s, "Let's Get It On."

A hush fell upon the room as we all stared at Gold Shoes who owned the phone which was singing to us all.

She flipped her phone open, exited the room and began talking.

The fearless leader was spellbound.

"Was that 'Let's Get It On?'" I asked.

The women on the couch nodded in unison, with sophisticated curiosity and visual delight.

"Let's hope it was her husband," said one.

We just stopped the meeting then and there. After finishing her conversation, our friend returned to the quiet room and demurely placed the phone back in her purse.

"Well?" we all said together.

"Well what?" she asked, dumbfounded.

"Was that 'Let's Get It On?'" I said again, sounding more like a parrot than a homing pigeon.

"Yes," she said almost apologetically. "I just love that song."

"Was that your husband?" another asked.

"Well, of course it was my husband," she said.

"Do you need to leave?" we inquired.

"No," she said, "I'm fine; I don't need to leave."

"Is that just his ring?" I had to know.

"Yes, and he's threatened to call me when I'm meeting with the preacher, because he didn't think it was a good idea when I chose this song as my ring. 'Don't you know what that means?' he asked me. Of course I know what it means; I also know I like the way that song begins. It's my phone, my ring."

We could hardly talk about casseroles anymore, so we just resorted to eating—another thing we do really well and in unison.

When it was time to depart, I grabbed my phone to make connections with the family and see which direction I should head to accomplish pick-up.

That's when a friend innocently asked, "What's your ring, Susan?"

I paused before I answered. I was humiliated.

"Ding-a-ling," I said.

And for your various family members?

"Ding-a-ling. Ding-a-ling. And ding-a-ling."

I've never felt more like a homing pigeon before in my life. A homing pigeon without any lipstick.

When I have time, I'm going to have a mid-life crisis, buy myself some gold shoes, paint my nails red and change the husband's ring to Conway Twitty's "Hello 'Darlin.'"

Then I'm going to Vermont.

Mothers
Only Rest
When They're
Dead

Frequently Flying Through Life

Although I'm not a frequent flyer, I have occupied enough "you're not as clean as you think" airline seats to be familiar with the view from the small window provided for passengers. I always look for the men with the lighted flashlights on the runways below.

And I hope someone buys them a Happy Mother's Day gift.

For as I observe their behavior, I am reminded of the mothers of this world. In the heat of the day or the cold of the night, these workers are out there: guiding aircraft for take-off patterns, checking their watches for minutes which make or break the day, and overseeing the loading of luggage, as if to ask, "Do you have your carry-on?" or "Did you forget your lunch?"

I identify, too, with the stewardesses, rolling that cart up and down the aisle, passing out snacks and picking up garbage. The pilot is there to narrate the experience, as do mothers: telling you when you're leaving, when you should arrive, and how you should act on the way.

I'm even qualified, given my 21 years of mothering, to be an air traffic controller. Try to get four people to the dinner table without an incident.

All of my airline window musings came back to me recently as I sat on my gravel driveway in Perry, Fla., and tried to navigate the daughter through Alabama's Interstate system to meet her father for lunch, both of them some 300 miles away.

"This is Air Traffic Control. Do you read?"

"I thought he said the second exit," she related by cell phone waves which have saved the day on more than one occasion.

"I'm not sure there is a second exit," I told her, as I ran from the house to the car for a map which might better define the route. The connection was breaking up.

"Do you read me?" I asked, launching my air traffic control career.

"Mother?" she asked. "What did you say?"

"Never mind," I said. "Can you hear me?"

With that settled, I found City A and City B and mentally drew a line between them. This is probably elementary to you, but not for me: my eyes glaze over when I look at a map. It's too much information. It's like being in a mall with 560 stores. Where do you start?

"And where are you now?" I asked.

"You've gone too far," I said as I verbally guided her around, moved her to another lane, and did so without causing any incident of local or international concern.

"There's only one exit and it's probably No. 29," I suggested, "unless they've re-numbered the exits since this map was published, which is a little like moving the furniture around on Helen Keller."

"Do what?" she asked.

I was doing the best I could, sitting in my gravel driveway. The dog assumed I was going to feed her, and the boys started gathering around me on four-wheelers and bicycles, asking for drinks. I pushed the dog with my left hand, directed the boys inside with my right, held the phone with my shoulder and the map with my cross-legged Indian stance. Let me see an air traffic controller do that.

"I've got about 10 miles to the exit," the daughter said at 70 m.p.h.

"I'm going to leave you, but only temporarily," I said to her. "Your arrival should be at 12:30 Central Standard Time, and I'll be checking in with you before landing."

"What are you talking about?" she said.

I then watered the dog, and gave the boys enough caffeine to make them a nuisance.

Afterwards, I collected the map and the phone again, just in time for the doorbell to ring and, yes, it's time for the schools to start selling wrapping paper once again. "You'll have to come back," I said. "I've got to make the planets align."

Several minutes later, the daughter was at the intended exit, looking for the intended restaurant and the actual father. She found both and there was a deep sigh of relief in the Air Traffic Control Tower.

But it's all in a day's work, whether you're on the ground or in the air. I knew that this small exercise in coordinating traffic was just the beginning: now I had to mentally get both of them to their homes—safely—before my eyes could shut and I could prepare for another day of take-offs and landings.

Maybe that's what Robert Frost meant when he lamented, "and miles to go, before I sleep." And he didn't know a thing about planes, trains and automobiles.

Hoping No One
Has Those Pictures

I want to go to summer camp.

I want someone to sign me up, fill out my medical form, send in my money and begin packing for me.

I want someone to tell me that it's important to wear flip-flops in the shower, and to take my own soap-on-a-rope.

I want somebody to put stamps on envelopes for me, already addressed for home.

I want a good book in my suitcase, a flashlight and some pink pajamas.

I want five outfits, two bathingsuits, some long jeans for hiking, a bandanna and a beach towel. I want bug spray, sunscreen and shampoo.

I want forbidden chocolate and packages of chips.

I want to go soon.

This year, as I have read the array of summer camps available, I really resent this work world. I could be a better person if I took a couple of months off for marine life studies, karate instruction, plant identification, spiritual study and retreat, exercise and nutritional counseling, cooking lessons and scientific exploration.

You appreciate summer camps for kids, if you're not one. The very idea of having someone pack my clothes, and send me off with a pre-paid calling card is very appealing.

I don't care how bad the food is, as long as I don't have to buy it, prepare it or clean up afterwards.

In my childhood, I went to very few away-from-home camps, but Girl Scouting did lure me to a place—always on a lake—where the shade was plentiful and we became very skillful at going in circles in a canoe.

It was my first glimpse of the real world, I believe, with people outside my normal realm of reference.

Weird people, you see, were there. At some point in life, you meet these weird people. You go home and tell about it.

And somewhere, these same weird people sit around their own kitchen tables and tell about the weird people they met. (That would be me.)

Learning that weird is relative, is important. I need to remember that.

I remember muggy nights in bedroom barracks, and lights out at 10. (That was the rule, if not the practice.) I remember bedsprings that creaked and bathrooms that reeked.

I remember mystery meat, singing camp songs, roasting marshmallows and making crafts with little pieces of leather, finished with beads. I remember water balloon fights and getting bitten by exotic insects, with friends around to walk you to the camp nurse. It was air-conditioned in her office, and everybody wanted to go.

I remember nature studies, noting that moss certainly does *not* gather on a rolling stone, and that mushrooms can't be trusted. I paid attention to the birds and came to treasure God's shade and clear water. I remember hours and hours of pool fun with swimming caps required, and I hope no one has those pictures.

Even with all that vivid remembering, I'm ready to go back because there's something very comforting about someone else taking care of all the details: driving you to camp, worrying about you all the way home and all the week long, wishing you well and missing you much.

They call it camp.

And you won't like it until you're 40, when you realize it's more fun to go in circles in a canoe, than to do the same thing in a car or in the grocery store.

Hello, Mr. Chips

We celebrated the New Year by having our snack on the kitchen floor, baby and me.

It was neither a planned event, nor an experience in Japanese culture. It just happened that way.

I had been to the grocery store earlier that day, and watched as fruits and vegetables, meats and milk passed over the scanner. Then came the chips: plain for plain ole me, and vinegar and salt for the daring at our house.

The groceries came home; the baby came home; and I was not far behind. All the perishables were put in their proper place. But several of the non-perishables lingered on the counter until time allowed attention.

What I did not know is that while the chips lay on the counter waiting for me to find them a home, someone found them first. They became part of lunch and were then placed back in their original spot.

So when I grabbed the bag to fling it into the pantry, I created havoc as never before.

Chips took wings and flew out the opened end of the bag, covering the stovetop, the countertop, crawling under the refrigerator, sailing to the small dining table nearby, decorating both my purse and the diaper bag.

It was a big bag of chips, of course. The economy size.

And suddenly, all economic strides were lost in one felled swoop.

I stood there with my mouth hanging open in a most uncomplimentary manner, trying to decide where to begin the clean-up.

The baby, however, is a quick thinker.

He doesn't get chips unless the big sister slips them to him illegally.

So he attacked with a vengeance, as if he finally understood what manna from heaven looked like.

It takes a while to cultivate a taste for vinegar and salt potato chips. He grimaced and squinted as he chewed up the first one. Then he declared, "Mmm." And then with more enthusiasm, "Mmmmm." And so he returned to the floor, eating his way through this mess.

I grabbed the broom, which made the tea party all the more fun. He dodged the broom, and then slid toward it on his stomach, as if it were the most pleasant way to spend a January afternoon.

As I swept up small piles to deposit into the trash, he ingested other small piles which should have gone to the trash.

"You're going to be sick," I said in a motherly tone, to which he answered with the most enthusiastic, "Mmmmmmm" of all.

With chips scattered to the uttermost parts of the kitchen, I gave up on conventional methods of retrieving them and, instead, resorted to his animal-like crawling and chewing routine.

There I was on my all fours, eating vinegar and salt chips off the floor, hoping beyond hope that no one would come to the door or window and find me in this bovine stance.

The baby? He rather enjoyed a little company on the floor, and also a little competition. He perfected his chip collecting to accommodate his appetite, and I commented on his hand-eye coordination while giving him copious amounts of water to counter that pungent taste he had come to love.

That's when he patted me on my back and said endearingly, "Ma-ma."

To those of you who don't know, that means "I love you" and "I'm having a good time."

It did have a pinata effect—busting a bag for the treats inside. So if January gets especially blue and hard to handle, grab a bag and hit the deck.

If you do, someone may call you "Ma-ma" and mean it.

Ciphering in a Concession Stand

If you are really and truly a mother, you will serve time in a concession stand.

It doesn't matter where; it doesn't matter why; but you will find yourself behind a counter swatting flies, slinging drinks and trying to make correct change so as not to embarrass yourself before people who are one-third your age.

I knew the school year was off to a raring start when I found myself in a muggy concession stand, surrounded by chips and candy, boxed in by cellophane bags of cups stacked on top of filled ice chests.

The price list is never easy. Everything should be a quarter or a dollar just to make life easy for mothers. But since life is seldom easy, it would follow that concession stand prices will not be either.

Doughnuts are 25 cents but drinks are 50, and if you just want ice, I'll have to ask. Cookies are 2 for 25; lollipops are 10 cents; and if you want chips, we've got five kinds.

The most popular variety of candy sold in this concession stand was priced: two for 25 cents.

"Will you sell me just one?" a young man with big brown eyes asked.

"No, we don't do half-cents," I said, as nicely as I could. It costs nothing to be nice.

"I can't afford but one," he added.

"Then I'll buy both for you," I said, remembering that it sometimes costs to be nice.

This can get you in trouble in a concession stand. I once spent $6 on a child who was starving, hadn't had anything since lunch and needed a sandwich for dinner.

After $6, I cut her off. Her mother would be horrified, but we mother-types do this sort of thing in case our children appear like waifs before other adults and beg for money.

It could happen.

Numbers have always been more difficult for me than words. I can talk my way out of anything as long as I don't have to add.

So here I am sweating and swatting, and some well-meaning student asks me, "How many of the (2 for a quarter) candies can I have for $1.25?"

He probably thought I was staring at him in impatience when I was actually ciphering (like Jethro Bodene) while looking at his eyeballs. I thought I might have to take my shoes off.

"What is 10?" I answered quickly, pushing the buzzer and forgetting that I wasn't on Jeopardy.

"What did you say?" he asked, looking at me quizzically.

"Ten," I said this time, more confidently.

How many could he get if he bought a drink, too?

When he wasn't looking, I did invisible math on the wall of the concession stand and checked myself. "Six," I answered zealously, again to be the first to push the buzzer.

Soon thereafter, I found a right hand man for the remainder of my sentence in this concession stand. He wasn't much taller than my elbows and I soon found out that he was enrolled in elementary school.

Let me tell you: the kid knows numbers. "As long as I think of it being money, I can do it," he said. I eyed him suspiciously, as if I'd like to buy stock in him right now.

He'd listen to me take an order, immediately flash to the price list, and voice his estimate on the order.

"That's exactly right," I said, surprised the first time.

There was only one possible slip-up in the whole afternoon's volunteer work. He presented one eighth grader's change to him and the student challenged. "You gave me too much money." I applauded the patron student's honesty.

But my right hand man was right. He added it up again, orally, and delivered the total again—for both of us—as if he was on Wall St. and this was the Dow Jones Industrial.

"Well, he's right," I said to the honest student, as I patted in a congratulatory manner the student who was both honest and accurate.

"One day you'll own this town," I said to him.

"I'd rather have a big city," he said.

You go boy.

Once when the afternoon's sales began to lag, my right hand man began counting money: pennies, quarters, nickels, dimes and dollars.

"We've got $51.75," he said. Then he checked himself, "But I'll have to ask what we started with, and subtract that."

I smiled proudly, and I'm not his mama.

"If you were in sales," I said to him with lilting expectancy, "ten percent of that would be yours. Maybe 15."

I let the words hang over his head as I watched with glee while the wheels turned, and chi-chinging noises went off in his cash-register-head, as he envisioned himself in a vault surrounded by money or driving the latest sports car with a convertible top.

It was a delicious moment among the doughnuts.

A little boy with a big future.

I had only one bad thought: One day, he'll probably be my landlord.

Going Once, Going Twice

I belong to an organization which has an annual holiday auction as its lone fundraiser. None of us want to sell cookbooks or raffle tickets on a toolbox, so many years ago, we decided upon an auction.

But it's a fundraiser with a twist: we bake, craft or purchase items totaling at least $25 and offer them at auction. Then we buy other friends' items to support the cause.

"Aren't we just recycling our money?" I asked, with a faraway look, while sitting next to the treasurer of the group.

"Exactly," she said, nodding in agreement while laughing at the sentiment.

"Couldn't we each contribute $50 and have the same outcome?" I wondered aloud, with furrowed brow because math leaves me with that expression.

"Yes," she said, confidently, "but it would require less time and aggravation, and you know how women love projects that take time and aggravation."

She was right. There's not a man on the planet who would bake for three hours, wrap loaves in plastic and tie with them a ribbon, just to see them leave the table for $3 or less.

Nope, men couldn't do it. Men wouldn't do it. If they baked, you'd have purchase a loaf for $100 and agree to change their transmission fluid.

But we women put our hearts on the table, wrapped in ribbons, scented with potpourri, warm from the oven, and let others haggle over the dollars and cents.

Honestly, we're not very good at it.

We know the current market value for every item presented, and are always looking for a good deal. "I can make that for $2," I'm sure someone was saying as hot chocolate mix found its way to a new cupboard.

Plus, we get all tangled up in family ties which never, ever leave us—no matter how far we travel, or how hard we try to distance ourselves.

For example, (in the dialogue which follows, the names have been changed to protect the guilty):

"Hannah has a dress that this purse would match perfectly," said one mother, offering a $5 bid.

Someone meekly offered $6.

"And she already has the shoes," the mother said, now at $7.

Another admirer politely suggested $8.

"But it would match Hannah's dress perfectly," the mother echoed at $9, in case we didn't hear her the first time, and the bidders went mute.

How can you bid against little Hannah?

Men could. Men would.

If Hannah's father had said, "Hannah has a purse this would match perfectly" (and clearly this is an imperfect example, for Hannah's father wouldn't know that she had a dress or the shoes), his $5 bid would be countered by a friendly challenge from afar.

"Well, then, I'll bid $50 dollars," his testosterone-influenced friend would shout. "Let's see how much Hannah means to you now."

With such a challenge before him, Hannah's father would surely say, "$75," for he couldn't be perceived as being cheesy and upping the bid by a mere $5. This is how auctions work when they are successful. They prey upon a person's need to be important.

Us girls? We just enjoy each others' company; we have nothing to prove, and no energy for proving anything because we've been baking for two days.

So when at $14 in the bidding process, a wife admits, "It's Freddy's birthday and this sour cream pound cake would be perfect," we bid no more.

She needs it; we want her to have it.

And when Jamie buys her own velour afghan back, we pause to ask, "Didn't you bring this?"

"Yeah," she says. "I really like it."

"Don't you know where to get another one?" we ask.

"Yeah, but it would take time to go back and get one, and I really don't have that. Plus, this is for a good cause."

Life is so easy among good friends. I enjoy sitting there, eyeing the treasurer and exchanging a glance: yes, we're just recycling our money.

But for the love of pumpkin bread, fudge and candles, we will do it again next year. Same time. Same format. Same friends.

It's what we call tradition, time and aggravation. And, clearly, it is how we define ourselves.

Damsel in Distress

In case you weren't there, I drove my car into a ditch in my futile quest for a parking space at the baseball park.

I don't know where my head was:

maybe I was making sure, mentally, that the headlines I had just left behind were straight;

maybe I was wondering what we would eat for dinner;

maybe I was considering how much hotter May could get;

maybe I wasn't thinking at all.

But when the front of the car dropped off about three feet, I started paying attention.

From my vantage point, I could see the husband in the dugout, poised to record statistics for the game. He didn't see me, which gave me two minutes to correct this problem without him ever knowing, but instead, all my tires did was spin.

I got out to survey the damage and felt unusually stupid. Feeling stupid is normal; feeling unusually stupid is worse.

"Are you stuck?" asked a kind and caring man to the left.

"Yeah," I said, with a considerable amount of humiliation.

He came over, looked around, and shook his head. "You're in there pretty good," he said. "But I could try ..."

About that time, two other team fathers started walking my way, ready to help. "Wow, you're in there," they said.

Then a coach. "Whew, you're in there," he said.

Then the husband. "What were you thinking?" he asked.

"I am so sorry," I said, and I was telling the truth. I was sorry I was stupid; I was even sorrier that I was caught.

The husband was being nice, given the circumstances, but I was rattled, given the circumstances. I just needed the world to stop for two minutes so that nobody could look at me, and I could sort through this mess I had created.

"I think the three of us can push it out," the husband said. We didn't have to cajole or promise payment to them; they just grabbed a bumper while I looked at them.

"Get in the car," the husband politely suggested as I stood there sight-seeing.

I dropped my purse and sunglasses, gathered them up again, and got in that car.

And I sat there.

"Put it in reverse," he said to me as if I should know such a thing anyway.

So I put it in reverse and sat there, again looking pleasant.

"Susan, you've got to crank it," he said.

"Oh, oh, oh," I said, as I fumbled around, spilled the purse, knocked over a drink and tried to crank that car. Of course, you can't crank a car in reverse, so I had to shift gears, both mentally and physically.

Then I looked up and saw the grimacing faces of men in panorama. There were three in my front windshield and one smashed against either side window. They had that pushing, might-have-a-hernia look, and I wished for the presence of mind to grab the video camera in the backseat, though none would have appreciated it, I am sure.

Those men were wonderful.

They pushed me right out, like they do it every day. It only took 60 seconds and no one delighted in humiliating me, although the husband did start walking away from the scene as if putting distance between him and the car would in some way separate him from all that is me, and all that is not good.

I drove slowly around the corner, waving to the crowd which was enjoying my misfortune, and the husband shouted to me. "Look a little longer this time for a parking place." The hard-working men grinned, and so did I.

Then I shouted back, "I'm leaving town and never coming back. But it's been fun."

He laughed; they wondered.

And that's the way I like my men.

Dragging My Heart Through the Halls of Perry Primary

On the eve of sending my second child—yes, my baby—off to school for the first time in his life, I realized that there were many subjects in my All You Need To Know About Life course that I had not covered before his fifth birthday.

We were leaving Perry Primary School following orientation, and he burped, enjoying the small explosion immensely. "No, no, no," I said, "you can't be doing that; it's bad manners. If you must burp, do it as quietly as possible and cover your mouth," I told him.

"Yes ma'am," he said, with a sinister smile I occasionally love and often fear.

Then I started wondering what-in-the-world I hadn't covered, prior to his debut in the real world without me. "Always shut the door in the bathroom and always flush," I told him.

"Yeah," he said, launching a repertoire of bathroom stories pointing to the bad traits of other friends—traits he would never, never, never imitate.

I was skeptical.

"You cannot run in the halls, or talk while the teacher is talking," I reminded.

"I know that," he said.

"Give it up," I told myself.

So he coughed, and sprayed my leg.

"You must cover your mouth when you cough so you don't pass germs, and when you use the water fountain, don't put your mouth directly on the part where the water comes out—everybody's germs live there. Catch the water in mid-stream," I said.

He nodded, with a blank stare, and looked like his father for a minute there.

"Will I still live with y'all when I go to Perry Primary?" he asked.

Oh yeah, break my heart while I'm driving.

"But of course. You may live with us until you're 30 ... but you'll definitely live with us while you're at Perry Primary."

"What if I get a spanking at school?" he asked.

"You'll get a worse one at home," I reminded, "but you'll still be required to live with us." Let there be no misunderstanding.

I tried to turn the conversation toward the colors and the computers, the numbers and the teachers, the stories and the music, the art and the ... playground. Yes, the playground.

Those are the magic words for this one.

We talked about slides, swings and monkey bars, discussed the long minutes he'd have on the playground, the friends he could romp with and the structures he could climb. Then we labeled folders and glue sticks, talked about lunch and snack, read a bedtime story and said goodnight.

"I won't be your little boy anymore after tomorrow," he said, and he was proud.

Since pride is a good thing, I delayed crying until I could fully enjoy it. While fully enjoying it, I wondered if I should have a third child at the age of 65. Then I wondered if I might be insane.

During the night, the four-year-old who no longer needs us fell out of the bed and sliced his forehead. We were up at 1 a.m. with ice and bandages. So I sent him to school with a backpack on his back and a bandage on his head. The backpack may fall by the wayside, but he'll probably be wearing a bandaid somewhere. Perhaps that's how they will recognize him.

He may think he's leaving me to go to Perry Primary, but he's actually dragging my heart down those halls with him. Just like my first child did; just like your child did; just like they all do, and always will.

They Were Singing My Song and I Couldn't Help But Listen

A couple of years ago, or so it seems, I brought a pink bundle home from the hospital and fell in love, in a new and different way.

A couple of days ago, I dropped off that pink bundle at a university campus in another state, and left with a broken heart.

On the surface, it was a day Martha Stewart would have loved for it involved cleaning floors, putting up a shower curtain, organizing a closet, lining drawers in a desk and a chest, hooking up Internet, moving furniture and meeting the neighbors.

When you look at it as a paragraph, it was a good day, a productive day, a successful day.

I kept telling myself: this is what I was put here on this earth to do, to raise this child in the way she should go, and then to let go. As a sentence, it's a good mission statement.

But when you leave that bundle, and all her bundles, 300 miles away and drive home, you start forgetting the paragraph and the sentence, and the ride home becomes a four-hour blur of old home movies and flashed smiles.

If you're about to go through this exercise of letting go of your own child, take my advice and don't turn on the car radio. Screen your music now for lyrics that remind you of anything that happened in the previous 18 years.

Since I banned all music I had shared with her, the husband and son picked "something country" on the radio and I was actually relieved because I don't like country music, and the daughter wasn't in jail like country songs lament, so I thought there would be no common ground upon which to trod. That's when Trisha Yearwood started belting out, "How can I live without you?" She said that 20 times if she said it once, as I attempted to be discreet about my sadness, underneath my sunglasses, peering out my car window to the right … seeing nothing.

Finally Yearwood finished wondering how she'd survive, although I continued to wonder about it, and lo and behold if some other country music star (who I don't know by name or face) began singing about "his baby leaving." Of course, his baby was surely his girlfriend, but mine had been my actual baby, and I was in deeper mourning than he would ever understand. If he had been there, I would have told him so.

I quickly changed the channel and landed somewhere else in radio land—anywhere else—while the son asked from the back seat, "Why'd you do that?" and the husband shot him serious looks from the driver's seat. It was an interesting tennis match of looks and glances, as Mars and Venus rode home in the same vehicle, with one small planet in tow and another left behind to find a new orbit.

On the Oldie-Goldie station was playing, "See you in September …" and that didn't make me feel any better either. Further down the dial, another country voice was crooning out, "You're gone and I'm left wondering how I can go on." Whatever happened to country songs about trains, trucks and prison—things that don't make any difference to me?

I really don't know, but on that day as I grieved from Alabama, through Georgia and into Florida, they were singing my song and I couldn't help but listen as I wondered where 18 years were hiding and how I would ever remember to set three plates, not four.

Now I'm listening carefully for a happy ending. I can't write it now, but I live in the belief that it exists and one day, it, too, will be music to my ears.

978-0-595-46763-1
0-595-46763-6

Printed in the United States
109585LV00002B/214/A